FAST GREENS

by
Turk Pipkin

Delta
Trade Paperbacks

A Delta Book
Published by
Dell Publishing
a division of
Bantam Doubleday Dell Publishing Group, Inc.
1540 Broadway
New York, New York 10036

ISBN: 0-385-31676-3

Book design by Julie Duquet

Reprinted by arrangement with Softshoe Publishing and The Dial Press

Manufactured in the United States of America
Published simultaneously in Canada

June 1997

10   9   8   7   6   5   4   3   2   1

BVG

FAST GREENS

MR —
Just a small reminder
that someone in
TX thinks you are
a pretty good father
too.

Happy Dad's
Day

Just Moi
6-13-97

P.S. met this guy at a writing
workshop in January.

Book One

———

Hope springs eternal in the human breast;

Man never Is, but always To be blest.

—ALEXANDER POPE

Introduction

IT WAS THE SUMMER I turned thirteen, and it had been a fat year in Texas. The mild winter was followed by a succession of tall booming thunderstorms, black with sweet-tasting rain, and the country, lush and green, smelled like the gardens of paradise.

It was a funny time: not long after man entered space, a Texan entered the White House, and though my pals stayed up late listening to the Beatles, they still wore their hair in flattops and spent envious hours in the company of their fathers.

Having no part in that, my days were spent in toil and grace on playing fields of green, hallowed grounds where one man, seeking his own salvation, would reach out his hand and change my life forever. Almost thirty years later, both the perils and the miracles that befell me on that incredible day shine as brightly in my mind as the Texas sun of my youth.

Tanned to the bone and sporting long, unruly hair, they called me the Wild Indian, but it was really just a joke. I didn't know about the world around me the way an Indian would; about the meaning of the stars, or how to follow forgotten trails and unravel the truth of hidden signs.

In actuality I didn't know much of anything but the game of golf; neither love nor hate, envy or pride, jealousy or revenge. I didn't know, but I was about to learn.

FOR THE THIRD TIME in five minutes, the big guy called me Skinny.

"Hey Skinny! Your foot's in my line!"

He had ten years and a hundred-pound advantage, plus one thick eyebrow that stretched all the way across his bony forehead. I moved the foot.

Beast drew back his putter smoothly, impossibly straight, like he was pulling a sword from a scabbard without the blade touching the sides. The putter face was square to his line at the back of the stroke and still square as it accelerated the ball toward the hole some eighteen feet away. His head remained perfectly still as the ball rolled a showering arc through the early morning dew, cutting a track that led to the edge of the hole, and disappeared into the bowels of the earth.

The ball plinked solidly in the metal cup. Without looking up, Beast dragged a second ball onto the same spot directly beneath his right eye. A long ash dangled precariously from the cigarette in his mouth as he repeated the putt perfectly, the ball rolling through the same damp track as the one before, and the one before that.

"Toss 'em back, Skinny! Before they get cold."

The words crawled out of the side of his mouth without disturbing the cigarette ash.

"My name is Billy," I told him.

Hoping to screw up his concentration, I scooped the three balls out of the hole and rolled them back at angles slashing through the single line in the dew.

Over on the first tee at the Pedernales Golf Club (pronounced Purd-n-Alice, because that's the way LBJ said it), my friend Sandy Bates cleaned his golf ball, paced, then cleaned the ball again. Sandy was a top-notch golfer, likely to play on the professional tour against Arnie and Fat Jack, and oh how I wished I were carrying for him instead of for this ugly putting machine. For once in his life, Sandy really needed my help. When he'd driven me to the course in the predawn darkness, for the first time I'd seen that he was afraid of a game of golf. Now to make matters worse, his partner March was only minutes shy of forfeiting this big match for both of them.

"He welshed, I tell you! Chickened out!" spat Beast's partner, Roscoe Fowler.

Roscoe was a snub-nosed, potbellied, sixty-year-old parody of all things Texan. His khaki pants were worn so far under his gut that you expected them to fall to the ground at any moment. And in the hazy morning light, his pockmarked face reminded me of NASA's lunar landscape photos taken from orbit around the earth.

"I know March; known him since nineteen and twenty-nine," said Roscoe. "Hell! He's probably halfway to Méjico right this minute."

Roscoe spit a big glob of brown tobacco juice—mostly on the green grass and partly on his handmade Charlie Dunn cowboy boots with golf spikes and little side pockets for tees. Unable to look away, Sandy gazed at the dark stain on the grass. With his stomach already tied into sailor's rosettes and other obscure knots, his blond face began sinking to a ghastly green.

Another man, known only as Fromholz, was there to referee this big match. Fromholz was not a man that you would mess with, and though I was afraid to stare, I found it hard to look away. His face was chiseled and tough, with one eye partially but permanently shut. His rattlesnake-skin boots and embroidered Western jacket probably cost a thousand dollars, but the New York Yankees cap on his head and the rolled bandana tied loosely around his neck were faded and worn. Turning his head to give his good eye a fair opinion, he glanced once around the deserted golf course.

"Be cool, Pops!" Fromholz scolded Roscoe. "Don't get your vowels in an uproar! I'm the man in charge and by my watch, it's two minutes till seven."

Plop went another of Beast's putts. Sandy winced at the sound, but his focus was still glued to the brown tobacco stain on the grass.

"Hell, Fromholz!" grumbled Roscoe as he limped over on a bum knee and compared his watch to the ref's. "You don't know shit from shinola! My Rolex says he's got exactly thirty seconds. And that's set to the atomic clock in Switzerland— *noocular* time!"

Like clockwork himself, Beast stroked another ball into the hole. Those balls didn't want to fall into the hard metal cup. No ball *wants* to go in. You've got to coerce them in, sternly but lovingly, the way Beast was doing it.

Again I dug the three balls out for Beast as nearby, Sandy gave a slight retch. For the second time in less than an hour he could taste the truck stop's greasy *huevos rancheros*—eggs with peppers and hot sauce—which were contemplating a jail break from his stomach. Worse yet, he could taste another bitter defeat at the hands of Beast the golf monster.

Just as Sandy started to gag, we heard a car gunning over the hill to the near-empty parking lot. Sandy swallowed hard and the *huevos* went back down to *huevos* land. Roscoe swallowed too; an eye-opening, belly-aching gulp of liquid chew. On the green, Beast's head jerked up as he hit another putt. The long ash from his cigarette fell softly to the earth as the ball spun off the edge of the hole.

"Shit!" we all said in unison as, wide-eyed, we saw it roaring at us: a shiny new finless and *driverless* '65 Coupe de Ville, its gunning motor racing with the devil. Without slowing, the big car jumped the curb and plowed through the wet turf that was our only miserable defense. I tried to run but my legs refused to obey, leaving me frozen in the path of the out-of-control car. It was already too late to scream.

A vision of road kill flashed into my mind—all the putrefied deer, skunks and armadillos I'd seen bloated by the side of the Texas roads. The vision vanished when at the last possible moment the car braked hard and slid sideways, skidding smoothly to a halt beside our huddled group.

I checked the front of my pants, then breathed a sigh of relief.

The window was down and Hank Williams was singing indifferently from somewhere inside the empty car. Then, like a jack-in-the-box, a shaggy gray head popped quickly into view from below the dash.

"Dropped my donut!" the man said. "Darn thing started rollin' on me."

The heavy steel door glided open and out hopped Mr. William March, flashing eyes, smart mouth, and grinning like a fool.

"The years came down, in crawling pain," sang March, twisting

Hank's song with his own words. *"You lied and lied, I went insane."*

"Morning gents!" he intoned loudly above the music. "Looks like you all got here early."

The four of us stared openmouthed, dumbfounded, happy to be alive.

I'd met William March only twice, both times at the urging of my grandmother Jewel, and I had yet to come to any understanding of his true nature. There was some mystery behind his tired and smiling eyes, something devious or devilish, or both. It was like he knew what no one else knew, some nugget of knowledge that he could use against the rest of us whenever he chose.

He tossed me a half-dollar.

"Get my sticks, kid."

Slipping the coin into my pocket, I dragged his monstrosity of a bag from the trunk and strapped it to a gasoline golf cart. March leaned in the open window of the Cadillac, shut up the radio with a yank at the keys, and pulled out a greasy paper bag.

"There's mine," March sang. "Twenty grand! And what a grand twenty they are!"

March handed the bag to Fromholz, then snatched it back.

"Hold on, cowboy! I almost forgot."

He reached into the bag and pulled out a partially squished jelly donut with a hundred-dollar bill stuck to it. Peeling them apart, he shoved the bill back into the bag.

"That was close," he said. "I damn near bet my donut!"

Fromholz peered in at the jelly-covered money. "I don't think it needs counting," he decided.

In the meantime, Roscoe Fowler was fumbling through the pockets of his own bag, which I'd already strapped to another cart. Without disturbing the little blue-steel automatic that I had glimpsed in the side pocket, Roscoe pulled out two fat bundles of bills and flipped them one at a time to Fromholz, who snatched them from the air: two lateral completions; crippled quarterback to one-eyed juggler.

I had caddied before for what I thought were big money matches, hundred-dollar Nassaus with automatic presses, and Bingo Bango Bongo where pink slips for pickups passed from hand to hand and losers went home on foot. But the moulah in this match seemed more like Monopoly money than the real thing.

"Hold it!" said Roscoe. "How do I know our ref is honest?"

"Hell, you can shoot craps with him over the phone," said March. "Let's play."

Gathering round, the golfers assembled in natural affinity; March and Sandy standing tall at one side, Fromholz in the middle, and the blackhats Roscoe and Beast on the other. Unable to take sides beyond reluctantly carrying Beast's bag, I stood to myself.

"Nine holes. Best ball. Winners take all," said Fromholz.

Then he pulled out a yellowed scorecard that looked a hundred years old. Squinting his good eye at the faded nine holes of figures scrawled on it, he came to a decision.

"Roscoe, you won the last hole, so I do believe, after twenty-seven years, you still got the honors."

Subtracting quickly, twenty-seven from 1965, I came up with the year of the last hole: 1938. Unfortunately, I was not as strong in history as I was in math, and I was unable to place any particular event with the year in question. Likewise I had no conception of the clothes, the music, even the cars. With regards to 1938, I was nearly blank. The only image that would form was one I had first seen just one week earlier, an image that I could not get out of my head.

* * *

William March's secretary tilted her head down, peered over the top of her small wire-rim glasses, and looked me over from head to toe. Apparently I passed her inspection, for she told me to wait in the hall, then she turned and disappeared through a heavy wooden door.

The walls of the hallway were covered in framed photographs, all of people standing near drilling rigs and oil wells, all except one. Raising on my toes to the level of that faded photo, I saw two men dressed in dusty cowboy clothes: wide-brimmed hats, leather chaps, bandanas around their necks. One of them was holding the flag from a golf hole while the other putted. In the background stood two horses with worn leather saddles, and hanging from each of the saddle horns was a golf bag.

"Golf on horseback?" I whispered to no one. I'd never thought of that.

My grandmother Jewel had let me off here on her way to the beauty parlor—though for the life of me I could never figure out why Jewel needed to be made more beautiful. We'd moved to Austin less than a month before, and already she had her choice of several suitors. Despite that, her only interest seemed to be in Roscoe Fowler and William March, two men she had not seen in almost thirty years.

Shortly after arriving in Austin, Jewel told me she'd run into an old friend who'd asked if I would caddie for him. She assured me that William March would make me laugh, and was a big tipper to boot, an important point because I was saving every penny to buy myself a new set of irons.

I had already carried for March at the Austin Country Club on a beautiful Sunday afternoon. Jewel had been right; he did make me laugh, at least until he and Roscoe Fowler began to bicker and quarrel, exchanging deadly verbal darts the way I imagined desperate men might fight with knives. The round had started pleasantly enough, but on the back nine, with March three holes up, things started to get ugly.

"This friggin' heat makes my goddamn knee hurt!" Roscoe complained as he knelt awkwardly for a better look at a do-or-die two-foot putt.

"I thought your knee hurt in the cold," March answered.

"It hurts in the heat *and* the cold!" Roscoe shot back. "And it's your goddamned fault. It's all your fault!"

"My fault?" March protested. "You sorry bastard! After the way you screwed up our company, you ain't laying the blame on me!"

"Up yours!" said Roscoe, giving March the old one-finger salute.

I was beginning to think they'd go at it this way all day long, but Roscoe lost the match then and there by jabbing the two-foot putt about four feet past the hole.

True to Jewel's word, March was a big tipper. He even gave me a ride home and bought me a chocolate milkshake at 2'J's Hamburgers on the way. We pulled up to our little rented house in South Austin, and March seemed pretty disheartened when I pointed out that Jewel's car wasn't in the driveway. I got out, thanked him for the tip and the milkshake, and went inside. A half hour later, I peeked out the window and March was still sitting there in his big Cadillac, just staring up at the house.

That night at the dinner table, I hadn't even said grace before Jewel started pestering me for details about the game.

"It was okay," I told her. "But I didn't understand what they were always arguing over."

"Well, they're probably just being pigheaded," Jewel told me.

"But if you really want to know, ask March. You might find it . . . interesting."

The pause as she considered that final word, combined with the slightest hint of mystery in her voice, suddenly seemed proof positive that March would allow me a glimpse of some secret of the adult world that lay beyond my imagination. And that was all it took for me to find myself staring at old photos in the hallway of an oil company.

The tall door of March's office swept aside and the secretary led me in. I'd never been in a real office before and it was different than I expected, darker, a little scary. The curtains were drawn tight and the room was lit only by a desk lamp that threw tall shadows onto the bookcases and walls.

Only half in the light, March was barely discernible from his big leather chair. Approaching slowly, I rested a hand on the big desk; it felt solid and heavy, and compared to the stuffy room it was cold as chiseled marble. The way it grew out of the floor reminded me of a tombstone. There was an odd odor in the room that reminded me of science class formaldehyde and dissected frogs, and I wanted to run away.

Looking older than his years, March produced a quart of Scotch from the desk drawer, opened it, and poured a glass half-full. Then he scooped in two heaping teaspoons of bicarbonate, stirred the concoction into a murky cloud, and drank it down.

"Scotch and soda, kid. That's what it comes to sooner or later. A man spends a lifetime washin' down greasy chicken-fries and jalapeño pinto beans with a hundred dry wells and it all comes down to Scotch and soda."

He held the bottle out toward me.

"You want a taste?"

I shook my head.

"Suit yourself," he said. "Have a sit."

Releasing his death grip on the bottle, March's focus swung involuntarily toward the cloudy dregs in his glass. I couldn't imagine what he saw in there, but his gaze reminded me of the snow scene in a crystal that Jewel had given me. When I shook it and stared through the swirling snow, I liked to think I could see through the windows of the tiny house to a happy family gathered around a dinner table, the father saying grace before he carved a big golden turkey.

"Tell me, kid," March finally said. "A good caddie can really make a difference, can't he?"

I looked up at his eyes and noticed he was smiling now. It was as if the very mention of golf had lifted the pall from the room.

"Yes Sir!" I told him. "A good caddie can read the greens like a book, and he knows the grain and the yardages, lots of stuff."

March leaned forward.

"You like golf, don't you kid?"

"More than anything," I answered.

"And for you—tell me if I'm right—for you golf is a pure game: physical and mental, joined together without any questions of right and wrong?"

I wasn't sure I understood but I nodded yes anyway. Golf is a noble game, a combination of uncertain skill and specific laws, untainted by ethical dilemmas or moral quandaries. The first twelve years of my life had been spent in hot dry West Texas, where the only snow was in my crystal jar, so golf was for me the one thing pure.

"What would you think of a man who cheated in a golf match?" March wanted to know.

I didn't hesitate, not on the one thing in the whole world that I knew to be true.

"A guy that cheats is lower than a skunk or a snake or a scorpion, Sir. I mean I've seen lots of people tee it up in the rough or miscount their strokes after a bad hole, but they're not golfers, they're just people with bags of clubs."

He shifted his weight, leaning closer across the big desk until his face was full in the light.

"I want you to help me cheat in a golf match, son. Would you do that for me?"

Not wanting to believe my ears, I looked away to the rows and rows of fat leather-bound volumes on the bookshelves.

"No Sir," I said, silently counting the books to avoid his gaze. "I couldn't cheat at golf, not to save my life."

WE MOVED TO AUSTIN, my grandmother and I, in the spring of 1965, and celebrated my thirteenth birthday on the day of our arrival. I had long hoped to trade the slow and easy small-town life of San Angelo for the excitement of a big city like Austin. My main desire, though, was to escape the memories of my mother Martha, who had gone out for cigarettes six years earlier and never come back.

Martha was only fifteen herself when I was born, a teenager with bangs and curls. Perhaps if she had sported long hair instead, I might have been able to hold her close. But my arms were too short and my cry too soft for me to grasp her young heart. Instead I turned to Grandmother Jewel, who fed me, changed me, loved me, and scolded me as her own, while Martha assumed the role of disinterested older sister. And since Jewel had been for many years without a man in her life, that was a role I was destined to fill as well. Ignored by a teenage mother and cradled by a grandmother still in her thirties, I was already the man of the family.

As I grew into my toddler years and beyond, Martha continued her life as before, idling away her time with dating and gossip, and sometimes caring for me while Jewel taught school. Among the few memories of my mother during those years is of

Martha constantly yelling for Jewel because I needed something or because I was misbehaving.

"Jew-el! The baby won't quit playing with the tee-veeee!"

Even when I was six years old, Martha still persisted in calling me "the baby."

"Jew-el! The baby's messing up my clo-set!"

Jewel would then come to correct the situation or else she'd yell to Martha to handle it herself. The latter approach generally elicited more protests until Jewel finally did arrive, or until Martha simply left the house, the town or the state, depending on how put-upon she felt.

"Stay out of the backseat of those boys' cars!" Jewel would shout after her as Martha bounded out for an evening of pleasure or work.

The only job my mother was qualified for was as an underage cocktail waitress in the one real nightspot in town, the Enlisted Men's Club at Goodfellow Air Force Base. There she continued to grow wild and restless until she eventually flew the nest, leaving her "baby brother" far, far behind.

Martha had been gone two years when she wrote from California to say she missed us; and would Jewel mind sending her clothes. That's when I knew I would never see my mother again.

Now Jewel and I had also left West Texas, and the only thing I regretted leaving behind was my nickname. While the other kids still wore the stupid crew cuts and greasy butchwax stubbles that their dads demanded, my long hair and dark tan had made the Wild Indian alias seem natural. But it did not follow me to Austin, and I soon discovered it is not an easy matter to rechristen yourself with a heathen name among strangers.

Sitting in William March's office that day, I suppose it was the Wild Indian side of me that felt so certain I could never cheat.

"Oh hell, I knew that already," March told me. "I mean you are Jewel's kid. That says it all right there. I was just testing you."

I smiled at him uncomfortably, not sure what he was getting at.

"No, what I really need is an honest caddie, not for me, but for the other team. There's a big match coming up, and I promised to find a bag-shagger for Roscoe's partner. The guy's a player."

"Who is it?" I asked.

"None other than Carl Larsen, state amateur champion."

I sat up straight. Carl "Beast" Larsen was the longest hitter in Texas, and he'd actually played against the pros.

Trying not to look too eager, I asked March about the pay.

"Oh, that's between you and your golfer," March said. "But if he pays you less than twenty, come see me about it."

Twenty dollars? The going rate was six bucks plus a tip that *might* get you up to ten. This was too good to be true.

March picked up a silver dollar off his desk and absentmindedly began to roll it one-handed across the backs of his fingers, sliding it back in a circle with his thumb.

"So whadaya say, son? Can I count on you?"

I was about to say yes, but hesitated for a moment. There was something in that last question I didn't quite understand. If I was caddying for the other team, why would March be counting on me? Then I remembered the twenty bucks, and I knew that at the very least he could count on me to do my job.

"Yes Sir," I told him. "Count me in."

For the first time since I'd been there, March smiled at me. He had a very memorable smile.

Now that we had come to that simple agreement, March seemed eager to talk about the big match and its participants. About the only thing he didn't tell me was who his own partner would be. Had I known he would be playing with Sandy, I'd never have agreed to caddie for Beast.

Soon Jewel was honking for me out at the curb. It seemed I had been there only minutes, but I looked to the big clock on the wall and was surprised to find that it had been exactly one hour, just as she had promised. Saying a quick good-bye, I bolted for the door before March could even get out of his chair.

I was climbing into Jewel's car when March came running down the sidewalk, arriving out of breath and almost out of words as we were about to pull away. Resting his arms on my half-open window, he knelt down so he could look straight across at Jewel who, after her trip to the beauty parlor, looked like she'd come right out of some movie magazine.

Not a word passed between the two. From either side of me their gazes met, and there on Cedar Street in Austin, Texas, in June of 1965, time stood still. I heard no ringing of church bells nor the sound of passing cars. It was almost as if the sun stood motionless in the sky. In front of my eyes the second hand of the heavy gold watch on March's wrist was frozen like a ship in ice.

Across from me, I noticed for the first time that Jewel's hair was different than I had seen before, though my mind raced to photos I had seen from her youth. I realized then that William March was lost in the sights and smells and sounds of a sweeter day, when life had been good and love easy. At first there was only sadness in his eyes, like sails hanging limp on a ship becalmed at sea. Then somewhere on the far horizon of their lost youth, a breath of sweet wind came rushing to the rescue of that floundering ship, flying across the blue and unfurling his eyes in a glorious recollection of a girl and a dress and a place so far away; and yet so close.

If that same memory shone in Jewel's face, it was also adorned by a single tear, which emerged slowly from the corner of one eye and slid down her cheekbone. Finally the tear fell free in the slowest of motions, then landed with a tiny splash on her hand in her lap. The deafening sound of that splashing tear was enough to jump-start time again, and as I glanced back at March, the second hand of his watch was ticking yet again.

"Glad I caught you," March told me softly, no longer out of breath. "You forgot your picture."

I didn't know what he meant at first, but I took the big folder he passed in through the window and there inside was the framed photograph of the two golfers on horseback. Unable to find my voice, I gazed at it in total disbelief that such a treasure should be mine.

"Golf will never be like that again," March told me, "and now you're part of it."

As we drove home, Jewel remained pensively quiet. During the drive, and through much of the evening, I studied the photo closely, wanting to discover everything about this wonderful joining of golf and horses—a new game from out of the old West. There was both mystery and magic in that photo, though I did not know how, or why.

I was reminded of a western I'd once seen on TV. A white man tells an Indian that the whites must rule the land because they know much more than the red man. With his spear, the Indian draws a circle in the sand.

"This . . . what red man know."

The Indian draws a larger circle.

"This . . . what white man know."

The white man nods in smug self-assurance.

"And this . . ." says the Indian, sweeping his hand across the vast horizon, "this is what neither of us know."

THAT NIGHT, UNABLE TO sleep, I lay in my bed gazing at the photo, trying to take myself back almost thirty years to that place. The story March had told me of playing golf on horseback was clear in my mind, but now the pictures were filled out by the moonlight outside my window.

"It was the fall of 1938," he had told me, "and the course practically glowed in the light of the harvest moon. The hard edges of the scrub oaks and scrawny mesquite trees were showing their softer sides, and there was no place I would rather have been.

"We considered it a private affair, a challenge between two drunken friends. What with looking for the balls in the darkness, it had taken us most of the night to play only eight holes, and with one par three to go, we were dead even. Roscoe stepped up to the ball on the tee, but halfway through his long, drawn-out preshot routine, the ball disappeared. The damndest thing: without Roscoe swinging the club, without the ball even moving off the little mound of sand that we used as tees in those days, it simply disappeared! I looked up to see if Roscoe was trying to pull a fast one, but he had vanished too."

March's voice, as if telling a ghost story, began to gather a hissing speed.

"A chill ran across my flesh, then it dawned on me. The moon had sunk like a stone into the gathering fog, dropping a pitch-black cloak over us, our horses, and the whole course."

To March, in the black of the moonless, starless night, it seemed futile to continue, but Roscoe wasn't having any of that. Lighting one of his stubby Camels, Roscoe smoked it down to a bright ember and set it next to the golf ball, which glowed in eerie red reflection. Then with the sudden sharp sound of forged steel on hard rubber cover, the ball again disappeared. Where Roscoe's shot in the dark had landed was anybody's guess.

They were contesting, March told me, for the position of chairman and head honcho in their own oil enterprise. And with that burgundy leather chair came the right to name the company. Damned determined to call it March Oil, he placed his own ball next to Roscoe's still-glowing cigarette. Guided by the scent of the lantana blossoms that surrounded the little adobe clubhouse beyond the green, March swung a smooth six-iron, knocking the ball out into the blackness where he thought the hole might be.

As I envisioned the story from my bed in South Austin, I could smell the lantana blooming outside my own window. And in my mind I could see that clubhouse perched on a hill above the Dry Devil's River.

March had described the sound of his shot: the simultaneous *whoosh* and *whack* vibrating outward only slightly faster than the actual flight of the ball. He told me that the sweet haunting sound of his clubhead making contact with the glowing ball was something that he'd never forgotten. He knew, and would always know, that his own shot had sailed more true than Roscoe's.

Finding his ball on the putting surface, March picked up a heavy iron roller and, in the dim light of the coming dawn, he smoothed out the sand between his ball and the cup. That's right, sand! In a futile attempt to find irrigation water for their new nine-hole course, March and Roscoe had drilled nine more holes, bored 'em deep into the earth; but instead of life-giving water, one by one the wells had come in gushing oil. Each one gave up a daily supply of West Texas crude, good for a growing country but hell on growing greens. With no other choice, they installed putting surfaces made of hard-packed sand. And to keep the sand from blowing away in the constant West Texas gales, they *watered* with a light mist of oil.

March's ball was one sandy putt from victory, but Roscoe's ball was nowhere to be found. I had witnessed Roscoe Fowler's perpetual complaining when I carried for March, and now I could picture Roscoe's increasing bitterness and panic, picture him stooping close to the ground, groping blindly for the ball, searching with desperation in the right rough, the left rough, short and long. I can almost hear him now, Roscoe the original curmudgeon, cursing the sun for coming so slow, the moon for setting so early, and the fog for staying so long.

"Oh mama!" Roscoe had cried out as he tripped over a root or a rock or a deaf armadillo, and landed on a prickly-pear cactus. "I'm in a world of shit now!"

But it was March who was really in a world of shit, because March was about to win control of Roscoe's life, and that could not be allowed. The senior partner picks the wells to drill while the junior partner picks his nose.

"Hey March," cried Roscoe. "Git out the Bird! Let's have us a drink!"

The Bird: Wild Turkey, Kentucky whiskey. March knew Roscoe was stalling but didn't mind giving his friend time for the light to dawn.

"I moved to the horses and groped in my daddy's oiled saddlebag for the bottle," said March, turning to catch my eye. "Those horses were my pride and joy, a necessity born of Roscoe's leg and my own invention. They liked to carry golfers, and waited untied while we hit our shots. My Appaloosa was born wild. I found her dying of thirst near a wildcat we were drilling in Big Bend; put out water and hay every day for a week till she'd eat right out of my hand. She never let Roscoe ride her either. When it comes Judgment Day and St. Pete wants to know did I have any friends, I'm gonna tell him about that Appaloosa.

"We huddled together, Roscoe and me, beneath a mesquite tree not much taller than ourselves, and passed the bottle back and forth. The gray-streaked dawn arrived before long, but didn't reveal Roscoe's missing ball. He took one last look around, planting his footsteps in the sand of the green in the process, and finally he conceded that the ball was lost.

"Fair enough, I thought as I stepped up to stake my claim. Two putts would have won, even three; but hell, I rammed it right in the cup for a birdie and the only key to the executive washroom of that soon-to-be-renowned ground-poking enterprise, March Oil! Hallelujah, brothers and sisters, hallelujah!

"Kid, I literally waltzed across ten feet of Texas to fetch my ball from the hole and, goddamn! There were *two* balls in there! We'd never thought to look in the hole, not in the middle of the night, on a dark par three? Who in their wildest imagination would have ever dreamed that Roscoe could've knocked his tee shot dead in the cup for a hole-in-one?

"Roscoe Fowler, the luckiest man alive: president and supreme head honcho of *my* company. Fowler Oil! Even the name was a bad joke."

TWENTY-SEVEN YEARS AFTER that historic shot, March saw the look of disbelief on my face as Roscoe Fowler, the very same golfing magician who had made a blindfolded hole-in-one, prepared to hit the first shot of their rematch. Roscoe's quick backswing was followed by an even quicker forward lunge, and he topped the ball so that it bobbled ignominiously to the ladies' tee.

"Christ, crud and crapola! I done drilled me a dry hole!" he said, letting loose a mighty gusher of tobacco juice that flew almost as far as his tee shot. "I don't suppose I get a mulligan?"

Pretending not to have seen, I averted my gaze and stared blankly at the long, untied laces of my high-top tennies. I was lost in a den of thieves. Roscoe could never have made that hole-in-one; it was impossible. Shoot, Roscoe couldn't even compete in a kids' competition. In the San Angelo caddies' tourney, any kid hitting a shot that failed to clear the ladies' tee was compelled to finish the hole with his fly down and his pecker hanging out. Not a comforting thought, but a good cure for a jerky swing.

Not having received any more answer than his request for a mulligan deserved, Roscoe stepped away, happy just to have his fly in the raised position.

"Well sir!" he trumpeted. "That's why I got me the best partner!"

Roscoe, it seemed, was not wagering on his own game, but on Beast's. And by wagering on Beast, of course, he was also wagering on me, betting a king's ransom that I would do my job honestly. And that's exactly what I intended to do: take the straight and narrow; carry the bag, clean the clubs, and keep my damn mouth shut. The first step of that task was to hand Beast his driver.

Wow! That thing's heavy, I thought. I'd be a dope to screw around with a guy who could swing that.

Though I had told March that I could not cheat, somehow I got the feeling he was still expecting my help. But it wasn't like I could simply step on Beast's ball when he wasn't looking. Golf balls will land in some pretty weird spots, but they don't fall into dimpled indentations exactly the shape of the ball. I could give him bad advice about the greens or the yardage, if he ever asked my advice, which he probably wouldn't. Beyond that I hadn't a clue, and that was final: I couldn't cheat; I didn't want to, and I didn't know how. March was on his own, and so was Sandy.

That was the best part of it.

Way over in one corner of the sky a few clouds still shone soft and pink, but they were just nature's little joke—the last illusion that the day would be anything but hot. As the rising sun began to show a growing speck of gold at the horizon, only Sandy had yet to hit his opening tee shot. His furrowed eyes showed how badly he wanted to start the match with more than a good drive, more than a great drive. Sandy wanted nothing less than to hit his ball just six little inches past Beast's tee shot, now cooling its round heels in the middle of the number one fairway, two hundred and seventy-five yards away.

Beast hadn't gotten it there with finesse. He'd simply flexed his big biceps and bullied the ball almost out of sight. Sandy intended to do it the hard way—with grace and skill. As he brushed by me on the tee, he spoke to me under his breath, like Babe Ruth making a home run promise to little Johnny Sylvester.

"Six inches past him," Sandy said. "Just six inches."

Gripping his driver lightly, Sandy squinted at the sloping green a quarter of a mile away. Allowing himself one wasted motion—a dry swallow—he set his mind to the execution of the longest possible shot with the smoothest, purest swing. The first move was contrary to all logic: a slight forward press of the right knee that effortlessly recoiled backwards, initiating the unlikely synchronized movement of the hips and shoulders, arms and hands, grip and shaft so that the clubhead moved straight back from the ball, conducting his turning body in a low-angled arc. His weight shifted imperceptibly to the right foot as the left knee bent toward it. Through it all, his head was still, his left eye fixed in an even glare on the ball.

It was impossible to identify the moment that the clubhead changed direction and the downswing began. Sandy's left hip had already begun to turn back toward the target, shifting his weight to the left side and accelerating his arms and the club with the potential—so far only the potential—of incredible power.

As the clubhead rushed toward the ball, Sandy instinctively performed one last crucial move: releasing all the wound-up power of his hands, arms and shoulders so that the moment of greatest speed was also the moment of contact with the ball, the moment the ball ceased to rest comfortably on its wooden throne, the moment the flattened-to-oblong sphere was suddenly flying at two hundred miles an hour toward its target.

The ball climbed above the full sun at the horizon while the clubhead continued its arc till it had circled his still-turning body and whapped him rudely on the right cheek of his butt. I knew he liked that little slap on the ass. It meant that he'd hit the ball the way he intended: perfectly.

When the ball began its reentry and descent, it had long resumed its round shape so that it bounced hard, then skidded down the middle of the fairway.

Perhaps my greatest asset as a caddie was my vision: I could see my employer's ball under almost any circumstance, a talent that never ceased to amaze me, since I did nothing to cultivate it such as eating great fields of leaf-topped carrots. Whatever confounded the vision of the other golfers and caddies—a background of white clouds, the blinding glare of the sun, a sky thick as soup with minuscule particles of Texas dust—they only made me look more closely and let me see more clearly. All of which meant that I was the only one to see Sandy's ball skid through the dew on the fairway and come to a rest just six inches *behind* Beast's shot.

But why should this contest have been any different from the hundred matches he'd already played against Beast? Since he was ten years old, Sandy had been competing head to head with his own personal golf demon, Carl "Beast" Larsen, and other than a few unimportant pro-ams or practice rounds, Sandy had been cruelly vanquished every single time. If it wasn't Beast's long drives, it was the crisp irons that landed ten feet past the pin and clawed backwards toward the hole. If it wasn't the snake putts from forty feet, then it was the smart-ass demeanor, that twisted sneer or the constant dangling cigarette. Sandy hated it all; the whole overwrapped package that mocked his own weaknesses, that made him look small, that exposed him for what he was to anyone who cared to see. Here he comes down the fairway, tail between his legs: Sandy Bates, loser!

Sandy badly needed to win this match; if not for the self-esteem, for the cash. The Professional Golfers' Association had announced that in August 1965—less than two months away—they'd be holding the first ever PGA qualifying school. The winners of this grueling 108-hole marathon would be given the dubious privilege of competing on Mondays for the available spots in that week's Tour event. Sandy intended to succeed at this tortuous rite, and to do so he needed cash. Ten thousand dollars—his potential share of the day's winnings—would do nicely indeed. But his dreams of the tour must have vanished abruptly as he arrived at his ball and was brought back to harsh reality by his opponent.

"Just six more inches, Sand!" trumpeted Beast as they stood over the two balls. "Six more inches and you'da had me. Shit!" he laughed. "Might as well've been six miles!"

Sandy sighed; it was going to be a long nine holes.

Six inches was nothing on a practical level, but to their egos it seemed all-important. Besides, Sandy would now hit first and Beast would gather valuable information from watching Sandy's approach shot.

Pulling his seven-iron from the bag, Sandy tried to muster his concentration, then failing that, he put his swing on automatic pilot. Once you've hit it sweet a few hundred thousand times, it's not that hard for muscle memory to hit a good shot. Sure enough, Sandy's muscles made a nice move at the ball, which sailed onto the green about thirty feet from the pin.

"Dumb-butt!" he cussed himself softly. "You gotta do better than that!"

I handed Beast the eight-iron he requested, and without so

much as an apparent second thought, he smote the ball a burning blow that cut a hole in the air. The ball landed fifteen feet long, then spun back furiously toward the hole.

"Wow!" I blurted out. "How'd you do that?"

"Well Skinny," Beast replied, "you just got to keep the grooves clean."

He handed me the new Wilson iron and a small metal file from his pocket.

"Every time I hit a shot with my irons, you're gonna clean out the grooves with this doodad."

The file had a square tip on it that fit neatly into the ground-out grooves of the clubface. I began to run it back and forth.

"Always perpendicular, Skinny; not at an angle, got it?"

"Billy," I said. "I got it."

March and Roscoe, in the meantime, were zooming back and forth in their carts, bouncing up and down across the rocky right rough in search of their balls. Roscoe had already sacrificed any chance of bettering his partner's score on the hole by chili-dipping his second shot and shanking his third. It was a pitiful display.

When March finally found his errant tee shot behind a stubby live oak tree, Sandy yelled to him, asking if he had a shot.

"No problema!" March hollered back. "All I got to do is catch this five-iron clean and get the ball up quick to clear that little tree."

Doing none of that, March jerked fast and hard at the ball, blading it on the sole of the club so that it rocketed straight at the tree trunk and ricocheted right back at him. With shortstop reflexes betraying a natural talent for the wrong game, he quickly dodged, leaping into the air and coming down splayed on one leg and one hand.

Hiding in a crouch behind his own cart, Roscoe burst out laughing.

"Ha! You almost shot yourself in the foot, old Poot! Lucky we got us a couple of sharks to help us out."

But the sharks, now strolling toward the green, were too perplexed by this inept display to even circle the bait, much less each other. In a partner's best ball, the team uses the lowest of their two scores on each hole. The higher score is disregarded. If Beast made three, it didn't matter if Roscoe shot nine or sixteen or withdrew, just as March needn't even tee one up if he was certain Sandy could make an eagle. The chances of Roscoe or March bettering their partners on just one hole seemed about as likely as snow on the Fourth of July. So as far as we could tell, it was just one more head-to-head match between the two young guns; only this one was worth ten thousand bucks to the winner.

For me, it was worth something less. But even with the usually crummy pay, caddying was a job I took with great seriousness, even when it was not entirely pleasant.

Jesus! I thought, trudging along like a pack mule. This bag must weigh sixty, seventy pounds. I bet Beast has got a hundred balls and ten jillion tees in here.

To make matters worse, in the excitement on the first tee I had neglected to shorten the bag's strap and it was all I could do to keep it from dragging the ground. Beast, Sandy and Fromholz all moved quickly toward the green, and though my legs were long, their strides were longer. I slogged along as best I could, despite the heavy morning dew that coated the grass and soaked through my high-top sneakers and my socks. Both Beast and Sandy wore leather Foot-Joys, a fine waterproof golf shoe that could be taken off your foot and floated on a pond like a Volkswagen bug. Foot-Joys shed water like alligator skin. Roscoe's boots, by the way, *were* alligator skin.

The sun was just high enough for the long shadows of the trees to stretch across the fairway like giant fingers that clutched at my wet feet. I hefted the bag higher onto my shoulder, tried to speed up, and wondered if I'd ever dry out, or catch up, or understand any of this mess. I was a fool for participating at all: caddying *against* the only golfer I truly admired, caddying *for* the only golfer I truly feared, and perhaps still expected to cheat by an old man I hardly knew.

Near the green, when the others slowed for March to hit again, I caught up in time to hear Beast—who seemed anything but a philosopher—pondering the true meaning of the day.

"Why in hell would these geezers offer me a sure shot at one half of twenty grand just to replay some dumb-ass match from thirty years ago?"

"Mayhaps . . ." said Fromholz, "they figgered you needed some fast green, Slick."

The locker-room scuttlebutt had it that Beast had recently lost a fortune in personal markers on Benny Binion's craps tables at the Horseshoe Lounge in Las Vegas. March had mentioned that Fromholz was from Vegas, and I wondered if our ref might also be Binion's bill collector. Then I wondered if Beast, suddenly silent, was thinking the same thing.

"Maybe it's not that much money to old March and Roscoe," said Sandy.

Beast positively cackled. "Who are you kidding? The word is out their company's in the shitter."

Handing Beast his putter at the green, I took a chance with my own guess.

"Maybe it's not about the money."

Fromholz, the one-eyed laughing bear, had words for that opinion. "Kid, don't ever forget this: When a guy says 'it's not about the money'—it's always about the money. But keep up the clean living there, Boy Scout."

I was a Boy Scout. I liked being a Boy Scout. But I hated being called one.

I WAS SEVEN YEARS old when I first saw someone strike a golf ball. At the time I was knee deep in the muck of Sulphur Draw, a pleasant but smelly creek that trickled and splashed over small rock dams and harbored a never-ending bounty of red ear perch, box turtles and crawdads. From its bubbling springs near the elementary school where my grandmother Jewel had long taught classes, the creek meandered twenty blocks through the oldest residential area of San Angelo, and dumped into the North Concho River directly across from the Santa Fe Municipal Golf Course.

On the day of recollection, each of my slender hands had a careful grip on a fat crawdad, their four pincers reaching desperately but hopelessly over their heads to lock onto their captor. The struggle was futile. Like bare-handing bumblebees off of flowers and jamming them into a jar, or snaring horny toads without being struck by the blood spit from their eyes, holding crawdads was a skill I had by then fully mastered.

Looking up, I saw a man on the opposite riverbank swing a skinny bat at a skimpy ball that ricocheted off a concrete park bench and bounced into the water with a splash.

"Goddammit!" the man shouted.

I thought this was marvelous—a game in which my mother's

favorite curse played an instrumental part. I clapped my hands in glee, momentarily forgetting the two murderously aggravated crawdads who suddenly found purchase for their pincers, each grasping tightly to my opposite hand. Releasing them with a scream did not encourage them to let go of me, and there I stood—sinking in the mire—my arms flying willy-nilly, and the two miniature lobsters holding on for dear life. As I was about to go under, either dizziness or my shrieks finally disoriented the crustaceans and they loosened their grips. One after the other they flew thirty feet into the air, each landing in the river with a splash of their own.

Sucking on one sore thumb and one finger, I stifled my sobs while the man tossed down a second ball and took a poke at it. Alas, this one was doomed as well, hitting both the picnic bench and a pecan tree before splashing into the river like the crawdads and the first ball.

"Goddammit!" he shouted again, hurling the bat after the ball.

The bat made by far the largest splash of all, and the man gave a little cry.

"Oh nooo!" he moaned. "My five-iron!"

I was very good at interpreting the bad moods and hangovers of my mother, and I quickly concluded that the man wished to have his bat back. Plunging headlong into the murky water, I demonstrated that the YMCA's lessons had not been wasted. Swimming thirty feet to the middle of the river and diving to the bottom, I miraculously came up with the man's five-iron on the very first try. Then waist deep on the golf course side of the water, I tossed him the club.

"Thanks," he said. "Say, you didn't happen to see either one of my balls down there, did you?"

I had not, but I knew where they had fallen. Within two minutes I was standing in front of him holding two mucky balls.

"Well, these aren't mine, but I guess they'll do," he said, handing me a dollar. "Boy, you sure earned that one!"

It was absolutely the very first dollar bill I had owned in my life and I stared at it in wonder, as if George Washington had strolled up and handed it to me himself. As the man picked up his bag and walked off, I yelled to him.

"Hey, mister, whadaya call this game?"

We owned no television on which I might have seen a tournament, so for all I knew it was called goddammit.

"Golf," he answered. "If it's good to you, you call it golf."

A few minutes later my friend Mick wandered up. In the same grade as myself, but a full year older, Mick was impressed by the dollar but allowed as how I was going to get my behind warmed for the mud on my clothes. This thought did not deter me for one minute. I still knew—approximately—where two golf balls worth hard cash were resting in the mire. It took me no longer on the second dive than it had on the first to return with two balls.

"How do you know those are the same ones, Creep?" Mick asked me. "Maybe the river's full of them balls."

I was awestruck by the beauty of his logic. We fished out balls for hours and sold them for a quarter a pellet to the passing golfers, making a total of five dollars each (plus my original buck, which I refused, under threat of frog knots and burnout, to split with Mickey).

Bright and early that Saturday morning, while Jewel graded her students' papers and my mom slept the day away as usual, I took my six dollars down to Santa Fe Golf Course and purchased one well-worn club—a five-iron no less. The golf pro cut the shaft down to my size with a hacksaw, then added a few wraps of masking tape to reattach the grip to the shaft.

"You need to buy balls?" he called as I ran out.

I didn't even answer. I was already swinging wildly at the thousands of fat pecans lying on the ground, waiting for another foul-mouthed golfer to bounce one into the river.

SANDY LIPPED OUT HIS long putt on the first green, and Beast had only an eight-footer for birdie and a win. After his incredible display on the putting green I didn't see how Beast could possibly miss, even though he hadn't consulted me on the break (almost none) or the speed (very slow). Caddies hate not being consulted because it means the golfer thinks he knows more than the caddie, and that's often the case.

In this instance, however, it was definitely not the case, and Beast left the ball hanging on the front lip. "A freckle short," as March described it.

"Yeow," said Roscoe. "You shoulda eat more beans."

Without looking up, Beast elevated a middle finger in his partner's general direction.

" 'Cause that one ran out of gas," Roscoe explained.

What Beast didn't know, what Roscoe didn't know, what I didn't know either was *why* the putt came up two beans short. Although the course was closed for weekly maintenance, the grass on the practice green had been mowed incredibly short and the base had seemed dry and firm. But this green was almost mushy, as if it had been soaked overnight, and the grass was grown out like three days of scruffy beard. Confused, I looked toward March. He was wearing another of his big grins and shaking hands with Sandy as if it were all a part of his plan.

"After one hole," proclaimed Fromholz, "the match is even-steven."

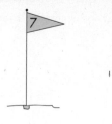

ONCE I HAD DISCOVERED the game and purchased my first precious club, I began to study the wide variety of golf swings at Santa Fe Golf Course. I loved the very idea of golf, the spiritual image of the ball in flight: each shot a tiny sputnik—the golfer both the astronaut and the rocket—hurtling through space and overcoming, however briefly, the grasping hands of gravity, breaking free as the earth passes below in a blur of trees and water.

The reality of the game, however, turned out to be quite different. The simple truth is that the crystal-clear image of a ball in flight is achieved only through boring, plodding work: long, monotonous hours of trial and error highlighted by exhilarating glimpses of success. The ball does not wish to leave the earth and has no interest in defying gravity. In truth, the ball is perfectly content to just lie there. Or, when struck a glancing blow by a young golfer of seven, the ball tends to scoot along the ground letting friction do its job. Friction, of course, produces heat, the result being a ground-hugging hisser then known as a "worm burner" but now referred to more often as a "bug fugger."

Our French becomes more proficient, but the dilemma remains the same: the reality of golf has no more to do with the idea of the game than a vista does a painting. Just as an artist may move paintless brushes on a canvas, a golfer may swing the club without a ball or target. But a canvas without paint, despite artistic intentions, remains empty, with no measure of the artist's skill.

So this cratered pellet, like a palette of paint, is really no more than a measuring device, an indicator that registers the degree of perfection of a golfer's every swing (not neglecting, unfortunately, the golfer's wayward thoughts in making that swing). To make matters more difficult, the ball also measures the wind, the water and even the specific gravity of the ocean's shore, commonly known as the dreaded sand trap. And for a proficient golfer swinging smoothly in a groove, more than anything else it indicates proper club selection.

Hole number two at Pedernales was what the locals called a little old par three. Nothing tough about it except that from the tee the green looked somewhat larger than a postage stamp but considerably smaller than an envelope.

Roscoe promptly threw out his honors and his back by topping another shot with a swing that reminded me of the one I employed back in my first year of play. When he lurched at the ball, Roscoe looked like a guy trying to fly cast a frozen turkey. You got the vague sensation that he once had a better swing, but perhaps couldn't remember where he kept it.

"Don't let it bother you," said Sandy, a nice enough guy that he even complimented his opponent. "You got a good short game."

"Yeah!" said March with a snicker. "Off the tee!"

"My partner, the jack-off king!" said Beast, enough of an ass that he even insulted his partner. "You could open a whorehouse and run it by hand!"

It was clear that Beast didn't view anyone as being on his side, not even his partner or his caddie. This seemed a lonely way to go about things. From the local scuttlebutt, I knew some of how he'd come to be that way, and even through my fear of him I couldn't help but feel just a little bit sorry for the big ape. No father was bad enough, but one who beat you must have been a hundred times worse. Though I craved attention, there are limits to all things, especially in what passes for love.

Roscoe had returned Beast's single-digit salute, but it did not stop the insults.

"What's your handicap, Roscoe: hemorrhoids?" taunted Beast.

"Why'on't you eat my shorts?" said Roscoe. "But first, hit your shot—*partner*!"

Without asking me for a club, Beast reached silently into the bag and pulled out his six-iron. Then he casually stepped onto the second tee and once again hit the ball a few feet from the hole. It looked like the simplest thing in the world.

Kissing his club and hugging it to his chest, he didn't wait for compliments.

"Oh you sweet little five-iron, you!"

Five-iron? Confused, I looked back in the bag. He hadn't hit a five; it was a six. Then it dawned on me. Glancing up, I saw Sandy—a funny look on his face too—as he exchanged his six-iron for a five. Sandy knew better than to choose a club by watching another player, but Beast was more than just another player.

Sandy made his usual sweet move at the ball; it almost took my breath away. The ball sailed as straight as a string, looked down into the hole for a moment as it passed overhead, and flew the green by twenty yards.

"Shit!" said Sandy.

"Shit has been mentioned," noted Fromholz.

Sandy fumed on. "I knew it was a six-iron! Beast, you must not've got all of yours."

Beast painted a shocked look on his hard face.

"I'm sorry, buddy. Did I say five? I hit six. Oh well, an honest mistake."

Jeez! I thought. These guys have got more tricks than a magic convention.

Simmering in his own juices, what Sandy needed now was for March to save the hole for their team with a solid shot right at the flag. What March gave him, unfortunately, was a Texas leaguer—a quail-high lob that bounced short and failed to roll on. Part of the problem was March's swing. Actually, all of the problem was his swing. March swung like the ball was a hand grenade with the pin pulled out. He had a choice of throwing his body over it or hitting it fast before it blew up. This time he chose the latter.

"Grow legs and run!" shouted March.

The ball did neither, stopping in the frog hair just short of the green.

"Hell, I think that ball's deef!" he said to me with a wink.

Sandy slammed the five-iron back into his bag and stomped off toward the green. Beast hurried to catch up and I hurried to catch up with him.

"Hey, Sand ol' bud!" Beast called after him. "Wait up!"

Against my better judgment, Sandy slowed and Beast drew up alongside him. "Say . . . you're not still mad 'cause I beat you in the state amateur, are you?"

Sandy was silent.

"'Cause it was just luck; like the high school finals at Muni. Hey, remember the Peewee play-offs when I chipped in from fifty yards?"

"Don't push it, Larsen!"

"Okay Sand, whatever." From behind I saw Beast turn his head to Sandy and flash a wicked grin. "So I got lucky and made a couple of forty footers."

"I said: Don't push it!"

"Calm down, Blondie. It ain't my fault you never beat me."

Sandy dropped his bag and wheeled on the big man, poking him in the chest with a sharp forefinger. Considering that Sandy was outweighed by thirty or forty pounds, this did not seem like a smart thing to do. Beast's Popeye forearms looked as if he could wring your neck like a dishrag, while his bony, stubbled jaw could bite off one of your limbs. Worst of all, the evil, smoldering fire in his eyes made him look like he was contemplating horrible butcheries on your vital organs.

But Sandy, acting so completely against his own personality, had taken Beast by surprise.

"Never," spat Sandy, "is a long time."

Without pushing his luck any further, Sandy withdrew his finger from Beast's sternum, turned, and was gone before the big man knew what had happened.

While we waited for Roscoe to hit his second shot, I picked up Sandy's abandoned bag and carried it over to where he was conferring with March. Sandy's bag, I noted, weighed about thirty pounds less than Beast's.

"He's right, March," Sandy complained bitterly. "I never beat that big shit. Either he gets a lucky break or I lose my confidence and fold in the stretch. Why'd you pick me to play him anyway?"

"Hey mama's boy!" said March. "You're supposed to be kicking his butt, not yours. I picked you as a partner because this is a grudge match: winner take all. And I wanted a guy on my side who's gotten the short end of the stick, someone that knows how to carry a grudge."

Indeed, Sandy's face was inflamed exactly like a guy who knew how to carry a grudge.

"Are you pissed?" March asked.

"Yeah, I'm pissed," Sandy told him.

"Good. Stay that way!"

Being pissed, unfortunately, was no help on number two. Sandy made a decent chip to the green, but he still had a four-footer for par. When Beast bent over to repair the deep hole his own tee shot had made in the green, he made a wisecrack about the divot reminding him of his ex-wife.

"You and every other two-handicapper in town," Sandy told him.

In a flash Beast was eye-to-eye with the source of the insult. I thought they might swat it out with their putter blades like samurai, but they just continued to stare. A fly buzzed around their heads, and still they stared. Long after Sandy should have turned tail and run, he *still* stared. And then I noticed their feet: one of Beast's oversized shoes was trodding heavily on one of Sandy's size nines. Sandy couldn't back off because somewhere under that massive steel-clad hoof at least one sharp spike was impaling him to the ground. Something needed doing.

"Beast," said Fromholz dryly, "I think that guy's trying to get your goat. Now let's play some golf."

The big foot came up slowly, like heavy machinery, and as Sandy's stare abated I realized that his face had just been frozen in pain. He limped away, two spike holes in the toe of his shoe, both showing spots of blood, bright red against the white leather.

Beast cackled a similar warning to the rest of the group.

"You guys think he's funny, don't you? Well, see how funny this is."

Replacing his ball on his mark, Beast putted out of turn. This was just the kind of rash action that Sandy had hoped to push him into. But that's where the plan went astray; Beast knocked the putt right in the hole.

"With seven holes to play," said Fromholz, "the team of Fowler and Beast are one up."

"Shit!" said Sandy.

"Shit has been mentioned!" added Fromholz.

SHIT WAS SANDY'S ONE and only cuss word. He also had a weakness for Tammy Wynette music and double orders of chicken-fried steak. His girlfriend's name was Darla. Like any true golfer's gal, she didn't play the game herself. One set of heroic feats per household, please. Otherwise dinner would never end.

I'd met him while caddying in the quarterfinals of the Texas State Amateur. To avoid playing Beast in an early round, Sandy had entered in West Texas. He'd asked around the San Angelo Country Club pro shop for a good caddie who worked cheap and they referred him to me. Since I was only twelve, he doubted my abilities but found the price just right.

Even at twelve I took the job seriously, unlike a lot of boobs who carried the bag backwards on their shoulder and cast their shadow on the hole when tending the flag. Partially guided—I like to think—by my expertise on the local greens, Sandy won his match five up with four to go.

In the quarterfinals at the Midland Country Club, he'd drawn a local oil-money favorite named Preston Deforest-Hunt, Jr. Having played at the course daily since he was seven years old, Junior knew it well enough to be a formidable opponent, even for a much better golfer. Unfortunately though, Junior was the occasional victim of a serious duck hook, the result of having learned the old-style hickory-shaft swing from his aging and doting father. A duck hook to a serious golfer, in case you don't know, is the golf equivalent of a Baptist preacher developing Tourette's syndrome, that dread and little understood neurological malady that makes one involuntarily spout the foulest profanities and bark like a dog. I once heard a respected golfer-slash-doctor claim that the only cure for either was a double dose of Thorazine, a shot of Old Crow, and a glass of Budweiser. Simultaneously.

Deforest-Hunt Senior was one rich oil-pumping son of a buck, but he had yet to find the right golf professional to cure his own infernal hook. To make matters worse, he'd taught his own weak game to his young son. Then having handicapped the kid almost beyond recovery, Dad had pinned all his hopes on Junior winning a prestigious tournament like the state amateur. So on the day of the match with Sandy, Junior was clearly out for blood.

Carrying Sandy's clubs, I was astounded at the consistently high quality of my employer's golf. Throughout the round he ignored the unlikely means that Junior utilized to get the ball in the hole. Sandy didn't panic, didn't choke, and didn't get demoralized by the miraculous recoveries from certain doom that his opponent hit on the odd holes or the long putts that he snaked in on the even ones.

"Well!" said Junior in his pseudo-British accent. "I *have* been everywhere on this course dozens of times."

Sandy ignored all this, negotiated the course with long drives and crisp irons and trusted in the fact that, since he was the better golfer, he was bound to win. He was two down with two holes to go when Deforest-Hunt Senior showed up to watch the product of his loins and inheritor of his own faulty golf skills kick some lower-class butt. But Dad's very presence reminded his offspring of all those early golf lessons, and Junior suddenly remembered how to duck hook the ball. Sandy won the last two holes and the playoff on number one.

The semifinals were at Fort Worth's famed Colonial, a long trip on the train that still carried passengers twice a week east and west from San Angelo. Jewel had a teacher's seminar that weekend, but put her trust in me by letting me go alone (with Sandy meeting me at the station in Fort Worth).

I didn't get a chance to study the course because the train arrived only the evening before, but it mattered little, as Sandy's opponent was a stiff, unable to work the ball under the big oaks (now dead but not forgotten) that used to overhang Colonial's greens. On the way to winning seven and six, Sandy taught me more about golf than I'd ever known there was to learn.

He taught me how to read the grain of the greens by the angle of the sun and the cut at the cup, how to tell the differences between bent grass (slick putting but lots of bite) and Bermuda (slow putting but bounding approaches), how not to be fooled by the mower cut, and on short putts how to listen for the ball to drop before moving my head. He told me to chip uphill with less loft and downhill with more, and never to hit a driver from the fairway when the grass is leaning toward the ball and away from the green.

Sandy could name all of the great Texican golfers and he occasionally did so when walking down the fairway, as if he were in a trance: "Guldahl Nelson Hogan, Mangrum Thompson Trevino, Sanders Zaharias Rawls . . ." chanting their names over and over like a mantra.

"Who was Trevino?" I asked.

"*Is* Trevino," Sandy corrected. "Who *is* Trevino."

"Okay. Who is Trevino?"

"The guy who taught me how to fade the ball."

"A fade is easy," I told him.

"Not a slice, Brainiac, a fade," answered Sandy. "There's a big difference. A fade is intentional; a slice is a curse."

According to Sandy, the reasons why Lone Star golfers win so many tournaments include the diversity of the courses in the huge state, the ability to play in the constant coastal and western winds, and having to putt on both bent and Bermuda greens. More important, they have that infernal sense of moral and physical superiority that's brainwashed into all Texans at an early age, and a Texan's commitment to a life's pursuit that doesn't take place behind a desk or in a store.

In learning all this, I had no doubt that one day Sandy would join the ranks of those chanted greats himself. And he saved the best for last, finally informing me that he'd also learned to play the game by caddying. So there was hope for my game yet. I was in caddie heaven.

But my elation was deflated somewhat when Sandy returned to Austin for the finals at Morris Williams, a course named for the most charismatic and heroic Texas golfer of his day. Morris Williams was a Harvey Penick student who was the only player in history to win the Texas Junior, Texas State Amateur, and Texas PGA championships, and he did it in one twelve-month period. Sadly, his career was cut short when he was killed while flying a training mission during the Korean War.

Knowing this, unfortunately, was no help in convincing Sandy to take me to caddie at the finals.

"It's too far from San Angelo, and there's no train," Sandy explained. "Plus you don't know the course."

True, but not the real reasons I didn't get to go. Just as Sandy had known in his previous matches that he was the better golfer and would certainly win, he also knew that Beast was the better golfer and would beat Sandy in the finals. He simply didn't want me to see him lose to Beast. In a way, I suppose I didn't want to see it either. I had never seen Sandy lose.

Now I'd ended up a traitor, caddying for his archenemy, the evil Beast. Luckily, Sandy carried only one grudge and it wasn't against me. He'd proven that by picking me up long before dawn and fueling me up for the big match with breakfast at the Big Wheel truck stop. As we made the drive through the hills to the course in his beat-up Plymouth Valiant, we talked about everything but his chances that day.

When the early hour overcame me, I leaned my head against the window and watched sleepily as the black sky was imposed upon by a slender turquoise wedding band of dawning light, creeping ever upward from beyond the hills in the east.

I was jolted to attention when Sandy pumped hard on his brakes to avoid hitting a red-tailed fox that scurried across our headlights and off the road.

Wow, a fox! I thought. That's a good sign.

"Almost hit him," Sandy said. "That would've been bad luck."

I glanced at Sandy, his face lit up green by the dashboard lights. He looked spooked.

9

BEAST WAS TO SANDY as a timber wolf is to a clever circus dog.
Back when Beast was still called Carl, his old man owned a
driving range, which is to say Pop drank a lot of beer and collected the money while young Carl picked up the balls. When
you're in your preteen years and picking up and washing ten
thousand golf balls a day, retrieving an extra thousand balls you
hit yourself isn't much worse. So Carl grooved his swing by
hitting balls till his hands bled.

When Carl was fifteen, Pop went out in true white-trash
style, going on a three-day stinker and taking a folding buck
knife in the gut (unfortunately, it was unfolded at the time). The
bank took the driving range and Carl took to hustling golf for a
living. No matter how much money he won, and it was plenty,
he couldn't escape his trailer-trash heredity and always lived in a
cheap motel. And no matter how much he lost (he often played
the best at Hundred-Dollar Low Ball with equal side bets on
greenies and sandies), he never carried his own bag. He'd picked
up so many range balls as a kid, he didn't even like to pick 'em
up out of the hole. A caddie I knew once followed him at a safe
distance around the Austin Country Club where Carl was playing a solo practice round. My pal picked up eighteen brand-new
Titleists that Carl had left in the holes.

In typical Texas-schoolboy style, Carl got passing grades, despite the fact that he rarely attended class; the schools needed all the winning athletes they could muster. Thanks to the curve of the grade and to some nifty work with a one-iron, Carl was medalist in the state high school championship as a junior, but he was disqualified for gambling on the tournament. To make matters worse, that meant he lost the bet he'd placed on himself. Maybe it was the bookies who turned him in. In any event, the treasured first prize was passed to the second-place finisher, Sandy Bates. I heard Sandy threw the trophy into a pond at Morris Williams. He knew who'd won.

A couple of years later, in Knoxville, Nashville or Gatlinburg—one of those faceless, reporterless stops on the Southern beans-and-rice tour—Carl met a golf groupie with substantial backspin and bite of her own. It must have been lust at first sight, for after winning his first tournament against the semi-big boys, Carl married her on the eighteenth green. Not long after, so the story goes, Carl's new wife started playing midnight driving range with a number of other golf pros who began to refer to her as the Dragon Lady (supposedly in tribute to her fiery talents with lips and tongue).

It was the Dragon Lady who rechristened big Carl as Le Beast. Apparently they were quite a team. If Beast was in the finals of a match-play tourney, she'd slip him a late-night mickey, sneak over to the opponent's motel room, and screw *his* lightbulbs in and out all night long. Beast, having slept like a baby, never understood why he was winning all those final rounds against tired guys with limp putters, till one of them—desperate to get back in the match—confronted the jealous husband with the bare-assed truth.

It was a rare day in the history of match-play golf. Since neither of the players in the final eighteen actually completed the round, the winner of the consolation match was awarded the five hundred dollar first-place prize. Beast was resting comfortably in the county jail and his opponent was in guarded condition at the local hospital. The other guy's memory lapses cleared up after a few weeks, but his hearing was never the same. Beast had bitten off much of the guy's right ear but, lucky for them both, the crowd pulled him off before he could get the other one.

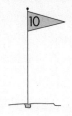

"ONE UP," SAID ROSCOE as we waited on the third tee for the greenskeeper to finish mowing the fairway. "Wanna press the bet?"

"You seem pretty confident," answered March.

"Confident? Hell, we gonna kick your butts! You *and* your pretty-boy partner."

"In that case," said March, pulling a sheaf of folded documents from his golf bag, "let's bet the whole kit 'n' caboodle." March handed the papers to Fromholz and the girth of our circle tightened considerably.

"What's that?" asked Sandy.

Fromholz cocked his head and held the papers in front of his good eye to look them over.

"That, Miss Curious, is the deed to a golf course, a clubhouse, a house, a barn, and some very old and tired oil wells."

"Don't leave out my daddy's grave and headstone. They're part of it," said March.

Beast perked up his ears. "Did I hear something about a golf course?"

"The Dry Devil's Golf Club," said Roscoe. "We built it."

"On *my* land!" said March.

"Aw hell, March! Don't start that doo-dah again. That land

was a company asset from the very first, just like my drilling equipment. We each made a capital investment."

"Your drilling equipment wasn't handed down to you by your father."

"How could it have been? I was a bastard. You gonna hold that against me now?"

"If you keep acting like one, yeah!"

March grabbed the papers back from Fromholz and waved them in Roscoe's face.

"Just sign the deed and we'll play for it."

On the big oak desk in his office March had rolled out a map of West Texas to show me what this match was all about. By myself I picked out points nearer to San Angelo, places I knew well: the parks with swimming holes and rope swings at Christoval and Knickerbocker, a railroad trestle high over the Concho River that I'd jumped from on a dare, and the abandoned U.S. Cavalry station at Fort McKavett. But March had to point out the dot indicating the golf course he and Roscoe had built in a crazed attempt to duplicate the links-style courses of Scotland, where they had learned to play the game.

"We went to Scotland in nineteen hundred and thirty-eight," March told me. "We were hunting for oil. A fat cat Scottish lord had come to Texas looking to shoot some big game. Roscoe and me, we steered him in the right direction. One night we were all drinking and telling oil wildcatting stories when his lordship informed us they'd been mining shale oil in Scotland for sixty years. Mining, but no drilling. I found that curious!

"We walked across Scotland for days. It was hell on Roscoe's knee, so we sort of limped from pub to pub across the Lothians into Fife, searching for seepages and uplifts and smelling the air for the faintest one-millionth of a whiff of oil."

I didn't believe you could smell oil beneath the ground, but March insisted I was wrong. They'd taught us similar such stuff in San Angelo at Santa Rita Elementary, which was named for Texas's first major oil well and where—Jewel's classes excepted—the three R's became four: readin', 'ritin', 'rithmetic, and royalties.

One day an old man came to our school and demonstrated the use of a doodlebug or divining stick. Holding the forked branches of the stick with upturned palms, stem pointed to the sky, he crossed our schoolyard until the base of the stick shot mystically toward the earth. The stick had found water, he told us.

The first graders were impressed, but we sixth graders knew better: we put our faith in science. That is, until Coach White gave Tommy Story one end of a long tug-of-war rope and sent him to the water meter at the street. Another kid took the other end over to the water cutoff at the side of the school, and they stretched the rope tight to find the run of the school's main water line. The rope crossed the exact spot indicated by the old man's doodlebug. He'd found water all right, a pipe full of it. Even the sixth graders were impressed. And with a branch from a beech tree, he told us, he could just as easily find oil.

Now March was telling me he could find oil with his snoot. He claimed that traces of iron inside our noses act as a compass—like a salmon's homing device—but due to evolution most people no longer notice.

"I'm just less evolved," boasted March. "To me the smell of oil is as strong as rhubarb pie."

A geologist is a great one for maps. March soon covered the one of West Texas with an old chart of Scotland, then he carefully traced their journey from Edinburgh around to the north side of the Firth of Fife, past the hamlets of Alloa, Dunfermline, Pittenween and Crail.

They were in the ancient town of St. Andrews when March finally picked up the scent. Triangulating with his nose and the very same map he was showing me, March got a bearing from the south of the ancient town and another from the north. On his last day of searching he planned to find a third and final bearing from within the boundaries of the town itself.

"I was so excited," March told me, "that Roscoe could hardly keep up."

Still waiting at the third tee for the mower to finish, I heard a second, more abbreviated version of the journey and how it led to the building of a golf course. But Roscoe's recollections were not so pleasant.

"It was cold as a well-digger's ass that day," Roscoe said. "Which was about the warmest it got the whole time we were there. Between my bum knee and three layers of wool I could hardly move, but March just hopped an eight-hundred-year-old stone fence like it was built yesterday. He waded across a road full of puddles and strolled onto a big green meadow that stretched all the way down to the waves. Then March sticks the ol' sniffer into the air and says he smells oil, lots of it!

" 'How lots'? I ask him, and he says, 'More than you can even imagine.' 'Well, where is it?' I say. And this joker points straight out at the cold ocean.

"Hell, he was pointing at the North Sea, and I *knew* we couldn't drill out there! Now here it is twenty-five years later and next week I'm going to the North Sea to drill for that same damn oil. When it makes me rich, I guess I'll have the last laugh, huh?"

"Well, Roscoe," March said. "The way I see it, you already got the last laugh. Don't you remember whiffing the ball?"

"Oh, hell, March, don't tell that again!"

Suddenly impatient, Roscoe began to yell at the greenskeeper.

"Hey, Manuel! Manuel Labor! We're waiting here like a bunch of hogs for slop. Fore, goddammit, fore!"

Over the loud roar of the mower, the man could hear nothing and just kept mowing. The course was, after all, closed for the day. The fact that March had slipped the pro a hundred bucks to let us play didn't mean anything to the guy who did the real work.

So Roscoe hobbled back to his cart and March told us about the big whiff.

"We're standing there staring at the North Sea when suddenly . . . *Yeow*! Roscoe grabs his shoulder and lets out a yelp like you never heard before. I think he's been shot for trespassing. We look around for our attackers and all we see is this odd white ball laying by us on the ground.

" 'What the hell is that?' says Roscoe. 'Some kind of aigg?' And I swear he turns his gaze straight up, searching for some giant Scottish bird. Hell, we were just a couple of hillbillies, but even I knew what a golf ball was. I knew St. Andrews was the spiritual home to the oddball game that had swept the States during the twenties. I just thought the game was a waste of time, but hell, so is life."

"That's the first damn thing you said was true," hollered Beast, who was pissing loudly into a growing puddle just off the tee.

March ignored him. "But Jesus, to hear Roscoe howl, to see that purple bruise, I was impressed. The ball must have been struck with an incredible force. And sure enough, out of the mist came four Scotsmen dressed like they were heading to church.

And tagging along behind them were four little tykes with bags on their shoulders."

"Caddies!" I blurted out like some damn fool.

March gave me a look, then he continued.

"Roscoe, doing a little St. Vitus' dance with the pellet in his hand, is about to spew some vile Mescalero curse on the Scotsmen when they beat him to the punch. 'Ha'e you no sense, lad? Ye mooved me ball froom its prooper place. Are ye trying to spoeyl me game, or are ye merely daft, eh?' "

It was a fair to middling Scottish accent that March affected, but Roscoe wanted to get to the point.

"I threatened to turn his hide bass-ackwards, that's what I did!"

"Yeah, Roscoe, you were always quite a scrapper. So when the Scotsman figures out Roscoe wants to fight, he starts in with the brogue about how he don't 'ken the coostoms' of our own land, but there in Links Land gentlemen settle their differences with a match of 'gowf.' But of course, the fella says it wouldn't be fair for a seasoned 'gowfer' to complete against a 'rank rookie' like Roscoe!"

Just telling the story is beginning to make March snicker.

" 'Rookie!' shouts Roscoe. 'Give me one of them sticks! How hard can the damned game be?'

"So they show him the basics of the overlapping grip, and we watch the Scotsman hit a shot that bounces onto what I figure must be the target, a big green area adorned by two waving flags."

"*Two* flags?" I ask.

"At the Old Course," Sandy had to explain to me, "some of the holes going out share big double greens with holes coming in."

I shrugged; how was I supposed to know?

"So Roscoe takes a mighty swing at the ball, almost drilling himself into the ground. He looks toward the green, then at the sky, and finally at his feet. Ignominies of callous fate, curses of obdurate execration, O scourging plagues of malediction—and goddammit too! He'd missed it."

"Big deal," says Roscoe from the cart. "So I missed it."

"Yeah, Roscoe, but you swung harder when you missed it the second time. I lost count about fifteen swings later when I fell on the ground laughing with the Scotsmen. But finally Roscoe hits the ball for the first time, a little top that sends it maybe twenty feet ahead. 'There!' he says. 'I told you I could do it.' "

"Tell 'em the rest of it!" Roscoe demanded. "I learned to hit it. I learned in *one* day."

"Well, you stayed up all night to do it," countered March.

Even Fromholz took an interest in the story. "Sounds like you were hooked solid Pops, hooked through the gills."

"We were both hooked," said March. "And that's how we came back from Scotland more interested in golf than oil. Since there wasn't a course within a hundred miles of home, we built one ourselves. Which brings us back to the deed. Whadaya say, Roscoe?" March pushed again. "Do we bet the course?"

"Not a chance. There's still oil under that land."

"Roscoe, it's all played out," insisted March. "Drained! Sucked dry! *¡Perdido! ¡Ya no hay más!* All that's left is my land."

"*Our* land."

"My father's buried there! What the hell are you worried about, anyway? You're one hole up and you got nothing to lose."

"Forget it; let's play."

Roscoe pulled a club from his bag and we looked down the third fairway. The mower was gone.

*　　*　　*

Easier on the eye than it is to play, the third hole at Pedernales Golf Club is a classic example of the strategic design theory of golf course architecture. The strategic theory, the wolfsbane of the casual golfer, was developed and refined by a long line of masochistic architects who were obsessed with their mamas and hated their papas. In order to punish the latter, they built golf courses which guaranteed that a golf shot lacking proper planning, let alone near perfect execution, would end up in a place from which the hole looked like a flickering star as seen through the windblown branches of a bare tree. On a strategic course the duffer has to go around the trouble and thus ends up playing a much longer layout than the pro. Sounds fair enough—if you're the pro.

What it meant here was that this short dogleg hole had a large pond yawning across the left corner of the fairway. The front side of the water was only about two hundred and twenty yards from the tee; the far side about two-fifty. Strategic intelligence tells the few who have it that they're not likely to fly the ball two and a half football fields. So the prudent course is to lay up short with a shot that lands high on the right side of the fairway and rolls down the slope to the bank of the pond. Any shot foolishly landing in the middle of the fairway might as well be bouncing off the end of a diving board because it's just as certain to get wet. On the other hand, a bold long knocker who successfully navigates his tee shot to the far side is faced with an easy wedge instead of a long iron to the bunkered green.

Beast, I figured, was considering all these pros and cons as he stared long and hard down the third fairway and scratched loudly at the stubble on his chin.

"Have a shot somebody," interjected March. "But don't hit the ducks on the pond."

"I don't see no friggin' ducks and neither do you," said Beast flatly.

"Right you are, Mr. Larsen," answered March. "I don't see 'em. I *smell* 'em."

"Bullshit!" mumbled Beast, testing the wind with a lofted pinch of grass. "Roscoe, you hit first, and don't whiff it!"

Some people shed life's capricious insults and embarrassing moments like a duck sheds water, while others are forever burdened by the heavy wet feathers of these past vagaries. Because Roscoe's mightiest blows had once been spurned by a lowly Scottish golf ball, he had taken great pains to learn to hit the ball properly. And a perfectly placed shot from the third tee at Pedernales finally proved that he could still do it.

With Roscoe's ball as insurance, Beast was free to go for the other side of the pond. Standing to one side, I could sense Beast's toes gripping the ground through his leather Foot-Joys. I could see the veins bulging in his forehead; each muscle and tendon tightened toward one object: power. It occurred to me then that I was caddying for the biggest, meanest, ugliest golfer that ever came out of Texas. When he swung I was sure that the clubhead had broken the sound barrier, but that mini–sonic boom we all heard was just the sound of wood on ball, a scorching blast that soared in screaming flight. Turning slightly to the left as if it had eyes, the ball landed safely on the other side of the pond, and bounded up the hill toward the green. From where the ball stopped Beast could probably toss it into the hole for an eagle.

Around the tee there was the smell of burning air, as if the devil himself had grabbed a driver and tried to knock his ball into a hole where it could nestle a little closer to home.

Once again, the pressure was on Sandy. Looking at his clubs, he considered the task facing him. His hand hesitated, this time between the five-iron and the driver: safe or maybe sorry.

March cheered him on softly. "Swing away, Sandy. Show him how it's done."

Sandy took out the driver.

It was a lovely swing, but just as he hit a light breeze came up in our faces. It was a lovely swing, but there was no sonic boom, no burning air. It was a lovely swing, but he wasn't Beast. The ball flew almost on the same track as Beast's, but it came down a few feet short of the opposite bank with a splash. The noise scared up a small flock of mallards who circled toward us, flashing their iridescent green and blue wings in a banking turn as they headed off in search of a course with better golfers.

"Po' little ducks," said Fromholz.

It was up to March. He pulled out a three-wood with a little apology.

"Us short knockers gotta use a wood just to lay up."

Taking the club back slowly as if he was in no hurry to win, March made his prettiest swing of the day.

"Most beautimous," said Fromholz.

But Sandy knew better. "Hit soft," he whispered. "Hit soft."

It didn't hit soft. The ball hit hard on the sloping fairway and bounced left, picking up speed and barreling toward the water.

"Whoa ball!" yelled March. "Whoa! Hold up now! Take a rest! Grow hair!"

But the ball didn't grow hair. It just kept rolling.

"Have a wreck! Hit something! Stop!"

It hit something—the water—and sank like a stone.

March began to holler at the ball as if it had stepped heavily on his bunions.

"That's a crock of fig-plucking rat-spit! Hey, ball! Why don't you take a flying—"

March might have given us an interesting tirade if he hadn't been cut short by a fit of coughing that blew up his face like a red balloon until the muscles in his upper body were constricted to rigor, his strong right hand squeezing the life out of his driver. We stood frozen in tableau as the color drained from his face, the muscles gave way, and the driver dropped to the ground. Gasping for breath, he stumbled toward his golf cart and pulled out his pills. Somehow he managed to get a couple in his mouth. Within seconds, it seemed, the attack was over, and March was once again looking and acting his own self.

"Goddam bum ticker, that's what I got." He took a deep breath and let it out. "Whew! Sweet Mother of Jesus, I hate that! Good thing we're just playing nine."

"Hey, old-timer," said Fromholz. "You look like you been ate by the coyotes and shit off a cliff."

Sandy pushed Fromholz aside and put an arm around March to support his weight.

"You okay?"

"Son," said March. "I'm just trying to hit every shot like it's gonna be my last."

"Listen," Sandy said as he climbed in to drive March's cart. "Why don't we toss in the towel?"

"Forfeit? What about your going on the Tour?"

"March, the game's not worth dying over!"

March forced a doleful smile. "Maybe not, but why don't you play like it is."

Just then, Roscoe sauntered over to check on March.

He ain't so mean, I thought.

"March. I been thinking," Roscoe said. "Let's play for it all."

"Roscoe, I as good as lost this hole already. That means I'm two down with six holes to go, my chest can't decide whether to explode like a well or cave in like a mine, and now you wanna play for my land?"

"Exactly."

"You're on," March told him. "Sign the deed and give it to Fromholz."

"Not so fast," said Beast. "Does the winning pro get a share of this crummy ranch or golf course or whatever the hell it is?"

"Pro, my ass!" scoffed Roscoe as he signed the deed. "I don't see no pro! Nobody around here but sharks and duffers and mama's boys. And I don't even know which one you are. So don't get greedy, boy—we ain't won yet."

MARCH WAS ONE OF those guys who even in a gusher year could never stroll past a golf ball in the water without trying to fish it out. With Roscoe's tee shot sitting pretty and Beast's almost on the green, you'd have thought his main concern was to take the penalty, get a good drop, and pray to Jesus H. Christ His Own Self for some wild hare of a hope at tying the hole.

But as the rest of us headed toward the pond, we were treated to the sight of March leaning out over the water, a wedge in his right hand, his left entrusted to Sandy who anchored him to terra firma.

"Hah!" snorted Beast, who didn't really like golf balls and did his best to hurt them bad. "Gonna be two down for twenty thou and he's sweating over a used Titleist. What a rube!"

Of course, I could have gone in after the ball, but I had already learned that a kid carrying a bag doesn't become a caddie until he assumes the decorum of the game. I would no sooner have waded in than I'd have told Beast I thought he was an a-hole. Golf is not a game about succumbing to temptation.

So, with Sandy proving himself at least some sort of capable partner, March successfully snared the ball and dragged it to shore through the goop on the bottom of the pond. Muck and all, he tossed it to me for a quick cleaning.

"Hey kid," he called. "What's your name again?"

I answered even though he knew it. "Billy."

March chewed my name the way Roscoe chewed his tobacco.

"Billy. I like that. Just like when I was a boy. Billy, you know why the pond holds water?"

"No Sir. No Sir, I don't."

"Duck shit! It coats the bottom."

I frowned at the slimy goop that the ball had left on Beast's towel and toyed with the idea of wiping some of it on his grips. Then I saw Beast fixing me with his evil eye as if he'd read my mind. The thought of him biting off my ear replaced the idea of doctoring the grips, and I turned to toss the clean ball back to March.

But then I noticed that something about March had changed. Both his cavalier attitude and his concentration on the game had suddenly vanished. He wasn't even considering the shot he was supposed to make. Instead he was staring toward the third green, almost in a trance. I looked to Sandy to see if something was wrong. Maybe March needed his medicine again. But Sandy's attention was focused on the green as well. The same with Fromholz, Roscoe, and even Beast.

And then I knew.

Standing next to the third green, silhouetted against the blue sky and motionless except for her cotton dress billowing in the gathering wind, was a very lovely woman. Even with my young eyes I could see that she was an exceptional vision of beauty. She was shaded against the hot sun by a slender parasol and her long fair hair was gathered loosely in a bun except for a few wild strands that played about her face.

For a long silent moment, the six of us stood sweating through the goose bumps on our arms, waiting for the mirage to disappear.

A low whistle issued from Roscoe's pursed lips, but it was March, speaking in reverential awe, who gave a name to the vision.

"Miss Jewel Anne Hemphill."

I could tell by the tone in March's voice, and by the look in both men's eyes, that to the two of them she looked exactly like the budding beauty of seventeen they first remembered from thirty years before. And the true wonder was that to me, too, this timeless woman looked just as she did in my earliest memories. I can see her still, leaning over my crib, her sweet smile stifling my infant sobs, her hair, long then as always, dancing into my stubby fingers, which squeezed tightly in an effort to keep her close.

Then another tender memory of Jewel rushed back upon me like a perfect dream. She had taken me on a picnic in the Hill Country one fine April day—April I know, because in Texas that is the month of bluebonnets. I was a little boatman surrounded by a sea of wildflowers: bluebonnets salted in patches of yellow and black Mexican hats, deep red Indian blankets, and stalks of purple coreopsis, all wavering like a painted canvas drying in the breeze. From my ship of quilted cotton, transfixed, I watched Jewel atop an island hill, a trick of the eye making her appear waist deep in flowers so that she seemed to grow out of the blossoms, her own floral-print dress floating among them like the living sail of a prairie schooner.

And ten years later I looked at Jewel beside the third green, still wearing one of her silken floral dresses, and the smell of those flowers and the sleepy hum of the bees came back upon me in such a flood that I almost began to cry.

God knows what visions rushed back upon March and Roscoe, but they were powerful enough for March to decline his shot and climb in his cart, leaving behind the ball he'd worked so hard to retrieve from the pond. He intended to get a closer look at the dream, but Roscoe cut him off.

"March, you prick! I still ain't hit."

"Who cares?" March shot back.

But Sandy had not hit his shot either. March snorted like a bull penned next to a pasture full of cows, but he managed to stuff his hands in his pockets while Sandy knocked his ball onto the green not ten yards from where Jewel stood, applauding softly as the ball landed.

Then Roscoe, no doubt inspired by the new gallery, hit his best shot thus far, a four-iron that sent the ball flying to the banked front edge of the putting surface. Though the ball appeared to be farther away than Sandy's, Jewel applauded more enthusiastically.

After rounding the pond with their carts, both March and Roscoe had to wait impatiently as Beast, his mighty drive resting a half wedge from the green, checked his alignment at least three times and flew the ball straight at the hole. A nanosecond after the ball left his clubface, both carts were racing toward the green.

"Christ! Give a guy a chance to follow through!" Beast called after them.

Whatever was about to happen at the green, neither Fromholz, Sandy, nor I wished to miss it. I quickly shouldered Beast's bag and the three of us hurried up the hill, leaving only the big man behind.

"Hey, kid!" Beast yelled at my backside. "How about my divot?"

Thirty feet in front of him I bent over as I passed the big clump of dirt and grass and tossed it back at him.

"Let him replace his own dang divot," I mumbled, opening perhaps the first crack in the floodgates holding back my dislike of the caddie's subservience. Those heavy tournament bags would never feel the same again.

BOTH RUSHING TO REACH Jewel, March and Roscoe skidded to a halt just below the green, jumped out of their carts, and started up the little slope. It was both childlike and wonderfully funny; one moment Roscoe ahead, only to be tripped up by March surging past, merely to be dragged back himself by Roscoe. Because of my long arms, one of my favorite kids' games had always been King of the Mountain. Coming off the starting line in the fifty-yard dash, I might have looked like a slow giraffe, and playing tackle football I was nothing more than a target for some overgrown linebacker who had failed a couple of grades. But once ensconced on top of a big boulder or sandpile I could not be easily dislodged. So it was with great merriment that I observed this adult version of the game between these two old rivals. I had heard country songs about playing the fool for love, but until that moment I'd never known the meaning of the phrase.

The greatest comedy was that somehow, after all their senseless jousting, both men arrived in front of Jewel at exactly the same moment. Standing side by side, their lungs trying to exact some purchase on the damp air, they doffed their hats, bowing low to what was obviously the single object of their hearts' desire.

"Miss Jewel," said Roscoe as March continued to battle for his breath. "Might I say that you are looking as purty as a picture postcard."

"Why, thank you, Mr. Fowler," she answered, turning to March for his compliment.

March took a short breath and let loose with one florid word.

"Likewise," he panted.

It was as clear as the smile on her face that Jewel loved it all.

"You gentlemen make me feel like I'm seventeen and the queen of the ball all over again. Now stand up straight and behave yourselves. You've no more manners than a couple of pig shoats; you haven't even introduced me to your teammates. Let's see, it shouldn't be too hard. Young Billy I know already, and you . . . you must be Sandy. I've heard a lot about you."

Sandy was clearly puzzled; he'd met Jewel several times and knew she must remember him.

"And this must be Animal," Jewel continued.

"Beast," he corrected her.

"Of course. Please forgive me; I'm not accustomed to such ferocious names."

Though it was obvious to me, somehow the others didn't seem to notice that she was kidding them with this act of Southern graciousness and aplomb. Of course they didn't know her as well as I did. March and Roscoe had not seen her from 1935 until just weeks earlier, an absence of almost thirty years. Of the other three men, only our ref seemed to grasp the game at hand.

"Fromholz," he said with a gallant tip of his cap. "No mister required."

"Well, Fromholz, to which team do you belong?"

"I'm the referee."

"How charming!" she gushed. "And who, pray tell, is winning?"

"The way I figure it, Roscoe and Mr. Beast there are fixing to go two up."

"May I watch?" she asked.

"Damn right!" "You bet!" said Roscoe and March.

So far Jewel had yet to say a word to me. And I was too surprised to say anything to her. I hadn't the slightest idea that she was coming to the match, and though I knew of her long-lost link to March and Roscoe, I'd never seen them all together, with the exception of another of the photographs lining the walls at March's office.

Not far from the horseback golfers had been a photo taken in front of an old wooden oil derrick: two grimy, smiling young men and a spotless woman between them. Where the years had been kind to Jewel, they'd been positively devastating to Roscoe and March. One crippled and the other all eaten up on the inside, they now seemed almost shadows of their younger selves, both beaten down by dry wells, broken hearts, and inside straights that didn't fill. In the photo they all looked close to the same age, but now you'd never really guess that Roscoe and March were only ten years older than Jewel.

As I contemplated all this, Roscoe, Sandy and Beast examined their putts.

"You want me to line it up for you?" Beast asked his partner.

Roscoe snorted. He'd rather have missed the putt than accept advice in front of Jewel.

"Suit yourself, old-timer," said Beast. "I'm gonna make mine anyway, and we only need one birdie to win."

But in Jewel's presence Roscoe was not an old-timer. Feeling his oats, he snaked a long putt up the slope that broke left two feet for every ten it moved ahead, straightening out only when the ball hit the bottom of the cup.

Jewel applauded with excitement, the fingers of one hand

patting quickly in the palm of the other. March looked away in disgust, not so much at losing the hole but perhaps at being so obviously bettered by Roscoe.

"Just once," March said to Sandy through gritted teeth. "I'd like to run in a long putt like that when it really means something!"

Sandy would have liked to make one as well, especially the one he now needed to halve the hole. His line was more straight up the hill than Roscoe's, and he should have known that his putt would break less. He should have known, but did not, and the ball slid past the high side of the hole.

"Two up with six to play," pronounced Fromholz.

"I could have made mine," said Beast as Jewel congratulated Roscoe with a peck on the cheek. "I could have made mine easy."

March dropped his ball and the babble and went all slack and sad-eyed as Jewel entwined herself arm in arm with Roscoe and the pair walked away as one.

"Honey, I just love a winner!" she said to Roscoe. "Do you know, you're shining just like when we ran off together in 1935."

"I could've made mine!" Beast said a little louder; but if anybody heard him besides me, you really couldn't tell.

ON THE THOUSAND AND something nights that my mother Martha stayed out till all hours toting drinks to flyboys for tips and squeezes, Jewel filled some of the parenting gaps by cooking, tending and tucking me in.

"Hush, Squirt. Go to sleep," she had told me till I grew too big for my britches and her little affections.

"It's too early!" I'd whine. "Can't I wait till the sun goes down?"

"Oh, you rascal! The sun's been down for hours. How about a story?"

Being a schoolteacher and well-read to boot, she knew all the traditional wolf, sheep, and prince stories, and by the time I was six, so did I. That's when I began to realize I could actually ask for whatever story I wanted. It didn't have to have a moral, and it didn't have to be out of a book.

Jewel just reached into her past and her family's past, pulled out whatever she thought was of interest or instruction, and wove a spell over me with her words. I still remember it all. Her grandfather, Adoniram Judson Hemphill; Adoniram, the Old Testament's Lord of Height; Adoniram, Civil War hero, Indian fighter, pioneer settler of Texas; Adoniram, who begat Elisha Judson Hemphill.

Elisha Judson Hemphill, self-anointed prophet, Baptist circuit rider, pioneer radio proselytizer, and Jewel's father; a stern man who followed the twentieth century from horseback to airwaves without changing his moral tune or his mind about heathens, sinners, adulterers, liars, cheats, back stabbers, or drinkers of backsliders' wine.

Despite being a preacher, Elisha Judson Hemphill was not a man of belief, being more of the disbelieving type. The list of things he didn't believe in was almost longer than my wakefulness. He didn't believe in dancing, drinking or the worshipping of idolatrous devils. He didn't believe in purposeless joy, ready compassion or the singing of anything but hymns on Sunday. He didn't believe in ice cream, root beer, penny candy or swimming, any more than he believed body heat was meant to be shared in the winter or aired in the summer.

And of course, more than anything else, he didn't believe in fornication. So when Elisha Judson begat Jewel Anne, she was living proof of the single sinful lapse of his life, one failed misstep intended to produce a male offspring. Though he had fallen from grace with a taste of evil fruit, and been punished with a girl, he became not a saint among sinners, but a sinner among men, determined to find the right track, to ignore his wife's cursed desires, and to raise a child more perfect and less sinful than himself.

So Jewel, begat of Elisha, begat of Adoniram, was admonished for sixteen years of Sunday sermons and dinnertime harangues on the major and minor disbeliefs: avarice and sloth, jealousy and greed, alcoholic fortification and bestial cohabitation. To me, the things he didn't believe in were like a roll call of shaggy unicorns, scaly-winged griffins and long-toothed dinosaurs. Jewel loved to tick them off to me one by one, laughing all the while at how she had once plotted secretly to violate each of his disbeliefs, starting with the world's number one and number two evils: dancing and drinking.

By 1935, the residents of both Del Rio, Texas, and its sister village of Villa Acuña, Mexico, had all had a bellyful of Elisha Judson. There was nothing the sinners would have loved more than to trumpet Jewel's fall in her daddy's face, nothing they'd have loved so much as to get his rantings off Acuña's 500,000-watt radio station, XER. So powerful was the station that its signal bled through onto every band of the radio. For six hours each day and night the only damned station you could listen to was that raving Baptist maniac, when all anyone wanted was a little bit of dancing music from New York, Los Angeles or Mexico City.

At least in the evening you could hear the brash nerve of XER's owner and primary broadcaster, Dr. Brinkley—the goat-gland surgeon. Brinkley entertained with his advertisements for transplants that guaranteed "renewed potency for the male patient and satisfaction for the wife who panteth for the running brook."

But no, it was Elisha Judson's god-awful preachin' all day long, and no choice but to leave the radio off, which, for some folks, still brought no peace. The unlicensed Mexican station was so strong that some people with a mouthful of cheap metal fillings could pick up the broadcast through their bridgework. More than once one of them just went insane from all that screaming in their brain. So Jewel knew better than to fall drunk into the street anywhere nearby, lest the locals paint her as Jezebel, people's exhibition number one in the trial of Elisha's self-righteousness.

Jewel's Cinderella ball would have to be in another kingdom, ninety hard miles away, in the town of Sonora, Texas. With four of her friends, Jewel set out from Del Rio one hot summer afternoon in a borrowed jalopy, willing to endure the rutted, unpaved roads in order to simply have some fun. And it was only when they topped a big hill, passing an iridescent turkey gobbler standing majestically beneath a sign marking the Sutton County line, that Jewel finally felt free of her father's foul breath and well-aimed accusations.

As they came up the valley of the Dry Devil's River into Sonora, bouncing along the dusty road and breathing through handkerchiefs, she began dreaming of the Prince Charmings who awaited her at the Wing Ding, southwest Texas's finest example of switching off the preacher and switching on the fun.

It was a big hoo-hah, too big for the county courthouse, too big for the high school auditorium, too big even for the town square. Only the largest buildings within fifty miles would suffice: the Western Star Wool and Mohair Warehouses numbers one and two. Each summer, right after all the smelly spring goat and sheep shearings had been shipped off to markets east and north, the ranchers of West Texas paraded into Sonora and begat a reverberating din of celebration and iniquity.

One of the barns was primarily for families: kids, old ladies and little babies. The main attractions were music, social games, lemonade, and a hundred yards of homemade food. To get in, you had to bring a covered dish of edibles. Twenty plates of sliced tomatoes and goat cheese or thirty hominy casseroles were not uncommon. There was apple bobbing, watermelon-seed spitting, and a thousand other activities, each of which, to an aspiring young woman of the world, was more boring than the next.

The second barn was for couples, ex-couples, would-be couples, confirmed bachelors, gamblers, whores, and other sinners too numerous to mention. To get into the main barn, you had to pony up a case of beer or a bottle of liquor, usually homemade. Though Prohibition was two years gone, West Texans went on as

they had for years, making it and drinking it and paying no mind
whatsoever to whether the law or XER's Elisha Judson felt it was
a good idea.

None of Jewel's friends had the requisite booze or looked old
enough to get in. They didn't really care, though, for they were
happy to listen from outside with a hundred other young people
in the same situation. Jewel looked the age, or at least by proud
beauty and sheer determination she looked unstoppable, except
she lacked a bottle. No problem: she just stood there in virginal
radiance listening to the strains of Bob Wills and his infernal
Texas Playboys as they tuned their instruments inside.

Before the band had played a single waltz, a man walked up to
Jewel with two bottles in his hand, two bottles because his partner had intended to be there too. But their oil well, the sum total
of their future financial prospects in and on the earth, and yet to
hit pay dirt, was behaving strangely. Leaking a variety of noxious
gases, the well required careful tending.

The whim of a single cut of the cards had left one sorely
disappointed partner back at the drilling site, and sent one, both
bottles in hand, straight into Jewel's tony white arms at the en-
trance to that barn. Her skirt was scandalously scalloped just
above her knees and her hair was cut above her bare collarbones
in a loose Gibson the way she'd seen Joan Crawford's in *Grand
Hotel*. It was a stunning combination of cowgirl, virgin and
movie star. To a lonely oilman she looked like fun in a pair of
boots.

Her new escort whisked her straight through those gigantic
double doors into a whirling cloud of dancers and sawdust, ten
thousand dizzying turns an hour, drinking and laughing and
dancing like the dickens to a West Texas waltz. Several hours and
too many drinks later, Jewel lay back on the seat of the man's
pickup truck. Half passed out as he tugged at her clothes, she

stopped him in a panic because she couldn't remember his name, and then allowed him to complete her indoctrination into a whole new set of beliefs when he reminded her for the twentieth gol-dang time that his name was Roscoe.

AS I STOOD ON the fourth tee and watched my grandmother flirting shamelessly with Roscoe Fowler, I could not help but wonder, was he my grandfather? Though I'd never known my own father, I'd at least known who he was, known by my mother Martha's childish vitriolic reminders that if he'd only taken the time to marry her before he got killed in Korea, we'd have been rolling in Air Force pension money. But Jewel had never identified my grandfather in her many stories, and I'd always hoped it was because he was still alive and would one day step forth and assume his rightful role at Jewel's side.

But Roscoe Fowler—crippled, pockmarked, tobacco-drooling grouch—could he possibly be the one? I'd refused to believe it from the moment I heard his name and connected it to Jewel's confession of her deflowering. He couldn't be my grandfather. I refused to accept the possibility. At least until I saw them cooing and wooing and carrying on like young fools. Then I wasn't so sure.

Why do I need a grandfather, anyway? I thought.

After thirty years, it was pretty damn late to step back into shoes that long vacant. To hell with him.

Jewel must've seen my scowl because, after some moments of questionable merriment, she left Roscoe and came to my side.

"I brought you something, Squirt," she said.

I flushed with embarrassment at the baby name as she pulled a brown paper sack out of her large straw handbag. In the sack was a tall bottle of Dr Pepper and a bag of Tom's salted peanuts.

I opened the bottle with the buckle on Beast's golf bag, ripped open the peanuts, and poured them into the soda bottle. Before the resulting fizz could surge out of the top, I took a huge swig. It was cold, wet, salty and crunchy, and more heavenly than tasting stars, which is why we called it caddie champagne.

"Thanks!" I said, releasing a rush of air from my lungs.

Jewel took off my cap and straightened my hair.

"You look almost like one of the men, Billyboy."

Smiling halfheartedly at her idea of a compliment, I messed up my hair a little, took the cap back, and replaced it in its natural cockeyed position.

"What about me?" came Roscoe's voice from just over my shoulder. "Didn't you bring your sweetheart Roscoe nothing cool to drink?"

I hoped that she hadn't brought him a thing, but even so I had no intention of sharing mine.

"As a matter of fact, Mr. Fowler, I did bring you something," she said.

His paper bag, smaller than the Dr Pepper sack, was the kind you get in liquor stores. The thing that amazed me most about this new and wondrous city of Austin was just how darned many liquor stores there were. Everywhere I went it seemed I was passing a liquor store. I figured it must be something to do with the legislature, which met infrequently and drank continuously here in the state capital.

It wasn't so easy to get a bottle in West Texas. San Angelo was—and is to this day—a dry town, which doesn't just mean they suffer from a shortage of rainfall. Being a dry town means

you can't sell booze in the city limits. This prohibition does not
apply, however, to beer or wine, which can be had by the bottle,
quart, six-pack, case, jug, keg or truckload on about every fourth
corner of town.

And the prohibition did not and does not apply to the county
in general, although there are plenty of dry counties in the Baptist areas of Texas. In San Angelo all you have to do is drive
twenty feet outside the city limits and you'll find a whole slew of
liquor emporiums, "package stores" as they're known, because
they wrap your bottle tightly in a brown paper sack. It was much
easier to make such a purchase in Austin, unless of course you
were thirsty on Sunday, God forbid. Suffering and misery
awaited the Texas heathen with a faulty Saturday memory, and
since it was now Monday morning, Jewel had remembered to
make her purchase at least two days earlier. I disliked her planning such a show of affection.

The bag Jewel handed to Roscoe, by the way, was pint-size,
and so was the bottle of Jack Daniel's inside.

"Whoo-eeee!" said Roscoe, taking a peak at the label. "Jewel,
you beauty, you sure know how to get a man's attention!"

Roscoe unscrewed the cap and held the bottle almost to his
lips.

"Hooch for a smooch," he said, lowering the bottle for a
moment.

Jewel gave him a wet one and as I walked away Roscoe
must've taken a big swig because I could almost hear his eyes
swell up with the first taste.

"Goddamn! That curls my shorthairs," he said. "I'm about as
happy as a dog with two dicks."

The rest of the group had waited patiently while Jewel talked
with me, but this was carrying things too far.

"Roscoe!" hollered March. "Quit screwing around and have a shot!"

"Hell," said Roscoe, ambling over to his cart for a club. "I never seen a man in such a hurry to get his butt waxed."

I handed Beast his big black-headed driver and was chugging down the rest of my soda, when—whoosh!—I felt the wind from a mighty practice swing as it passed within an inch of my ear.

Spitting out a fountain of Dr Pepper and a trail of peanuts, I saw the club coming back for me again.

Whoosh!

Still mad at being superfluous, Beast was taking it out on the air and anything else that got in his way. If I hadn't ducked, he'd have thumped my head like a pumpkin.

Whoosh!

The club swung forward and—whoosh!—it went back again. I jumped back two giant steps and took refuge in the company of March and Sandy.

"Sandy, it's time to pull out all the stops," March was telling him in measured confidence.

"What!" Sandy hissed. "You think I been holding something back? I'm playing as hard as I know how."

March looked at him with a stone face. "I ain't talking about *play!*"

"Nice shot, Roscoe!" March added a little louder. Roscoe had whapped it out about two hundred yards right down the middle. "One more of those and you'll have it out to where Slammin' Sammy hit his tee shot in 'forty-eight."

Beast, stepping into the batter's box, perked up his ears at that.

"Where'd Snead hit it to?" he asked.

Having hooked his fish, March had only to reel him in.

Number four was a long dogleg par five with some sizable oak trees protecting the corner about two hundred and sixty yards away. March told us that Snead had cut the corner by going over the trees, leaving himself a mere middle-iron to the green while the other players had to feather in a three-wood or a fairway driver.

"Course Slammin' Sammy was a *long* hitter," concluded March, implying that Beast was not.

It was a valiant effort, perhaps the best of the three incredible drives Beast had hit thus far. Still, my heart cheered as his tee shot came up short of his goal, slammed into the ten percent of tree that wasn't air, and fell down beneath the overhanging branches.

"Son of a bitch!" yelled Beast. "Snead never hit it over those trees!"

"Sure he did!" boasted March. "Of course, those trees were just saplings in 'forty-eight, probably a lot shorter then."

Beast's face began to rage into shades of scarlet. We all stepped back, except Fromholz—Dr. Cool—who stepped toward Beast, but not before slipping one hand into the bulging pocket of his jacket. It was not the pocket he'd stuffed the wads of cash into and it was not too hard to guess what he had in there. This guy took the referee job very seriously, carrying it so far as to provide protection for the participants. But March didn't really need protection. He wasn't even done yet.

"Oh, hell!" March said. "What a stoop I am. My memory's all screwed up. I don't think it was this course at all. Come to think of it, I can't even remember if this course was here in 'forty-eight. I must be goin' crazy—crazy like a bat."

"The expression is crazy like a fox," said Roscoe.

"Whatever."

If the first confession had served to pump Beast up, the second had taken all the wind out of his sails, and then some. He exhaled a mighty blast of disgust and even I could see that the physical danger was past. Beast simmered back a few steps, Fromholz withdrew his hand from his pocket, and March stepped up to hit his own shot.

The trick had been a marvel, but despite his tactical triumph, March hit his ball deep into the right woods. A minute later, the most unimaginable event of the day happened: Sandy hit his shot and I didn't see where it went. I was too busy watching Roscoe slip a hundred-dollar bill into Fromholz's hand.

"Ride over there and keep March honest, ref," said Roscoe in a pseudo-whisper, which wasn't much under a low roar.

Roscoe knew full well that March was little or no threat on this long par five, so I figured his main intention was to distract Sandy during his swing. But if Sandy had been bothered, he certainly didn't let on. Instead he picked up his bag and started down the fairway without complaint.

Guys whose concentration can't be broken never cease to amaze me. I carried once for Don Cherry, a famous Texas singing golfer who hit the ball sweet despite a lot of attractive requests for autographs and an occasional jealous husband. When I asked him how he avoided distractions, Cherry told me he used to hit practice balls with a lady friend sunning nearby in her birthday suit. Once he got used to that, the rest was easy.

"Jewel darling!" drawled Roscoe as they sat in his cart in the middle of the fairway. "Ol' March there is knee-deep in shit and coffee break's about over. And we know what that means. Back on his head! He ain't never gonna find that ball. Maybe you and I should run off to *Foat* Worth to celebrate."

Tilting his bottle, Roscoe toasted March's lost balls and then waited for March to give up the search. That Dr Pepper had run through me pretty quick, and with Jewel ten feet away I had to excuse myself for the woods. By the time I reached the nearest bushes, March had found his ball. From my new position I had a good view as he studied his dismal prospects, blocked from the others' view by the same cover I was using, blocked from the green by a row of trees and blocked from a rat's-ass chance of reaching the fairway by all of it.

Since neither March nor Fromholz saw me standing there conducting my business, it was almost like being the proverbial fly on the wall.

"How much did Roscoe give you, Ace?" March asked Fromholz.

"A hundred."

March took out his wallet. "Here's *five* hundred."

"You want me to move it?" asked Fromholz.

"Move it?" says March. "Hell, I want you to hit it!"

March handed Fromholz what looked to be a four-wood.

Alarmed, I turned back to the fairway to see if the others were watching, but they couldn't see a thing; I was the only witness. I didn't even know if Fromholz knew how to play golf. Even for a pro, getting the ball over those trees would have been tough with a wood. Fromholz took a couple of powerful practice swings, free and loose, then stepped up to the ball.

"Fore!" yelled March.

The group in the fairway jerked their heads up in unison, kind of like cows in a field. Jewel had taught me to think in such pictures, but I don't think she'd have been humored to be a part of that one.

Fromholz made a move at the ball exactly like each of his perfect practice swings, and the ball jumped off his open clubface and soared out of sight. I couldn't tell where it went, but when it cleared the trees Sandy started hollering and screaming from the fairway.

"Yeah! Yeah! Great shot! Go! Go! Yeah!" Sandy was only about four words away from being speechless.

When you see a golfer with a great swing, it sticks with you forever. To this day I've only seen about a dozen truly great swings, and they belonged to Sandy, maybe to Beast, to a handful of guys out on the Tour (not all of whom have been successful), and to Fromholz. Later on I learned that our ref had shown a lot of golfing promise until he'd been hit square in the eye by a golf ball. I'd hate to be the idiot who hit a ball that destroyed something so fine in a man as tough as Fromholz.

Zipping up my fly, I ran back to the fairway as fast as I could. By the remarks I surmised that March's ball was either on or very near the green; in two shots, putting for eagle. And Roscoe just couldn't imagine how that duffer March could have managed such an incredible shot.

I WAS BY NATURE neither a fighter nor a fink, falling somewhere in the middle ground of these dubious childhood achievements. I'd always made too good of grades to be hip, and I teetered precariously on the line of being a Goody Two-shoes, but I could usually be counted on to participate in a little group mayhem as long as it didn't cause me any physical pain. Most notable among these escalating instances of delinquency in San Angelo was a boredom-induced rock fight among a group of my sixth-grade classmates. I hadn't really wanted to take part, primarily because in the prebattle negotiations I was appointed captain of the geek team, which consisted of myself, fat Donny Ratley, and Clyde Eckhardt, the stutter king.

The three of us were sure to get pulverized, tenderized like a bad cut of meat. My ego was already injured by not being included on the team of the genetically cool, but when somebody screams "Go!" and the rocks start flying, there's not much you can do but dive for cover, gather an armful of ammunition, and start lobbing a few long, deadly bombs between the incoming salvos.

One of the reasons I liked golf so much was because the rules were so specific. There ain't no rules in a rock fight. Hopelessly outgunned, my army bruised and battered, and one of my troops crying shamelessly, a ray of hope broke through the clouds. A seventh kid walked up in a lull between volleys, and, unable to comprehend the murderous sincerity of the game, he wanted to play. Even though Larry Seebers wore thick glasses and threw like a girl, an extra body on my side gave us a remote chance of not dying a horrible death before the end of recess. But it was not to be. As I jumped from cover to claim him as ours, I was immediately buried by a barrage of rockwork.

"Larry's on our side!" the other team yelled. "You guys outweigh us!"

It was true. Weight was our only advantage. And never having been on any sporting team with the cool guys, Larry fairly beamed with complicity. My protests were answered with another volley of rocks and I was driven back into my hole. The only thing that kept the game going was that, mad as I was, no one in their right mind was gonna get within thirty feet of my long slingshot arm. Nobody, that is, except a geek in glasses who didn't know the game. Nobody but Larry.

"Here's what you do," his new teammates explained as they handed him his first rock. "Run straight at Billy, screaming as loud as you can. We'll do the rest!"

What a rube this kid was. Not questioning this idiotic directive, Private Larry ran at me, screaming for all he was worth. Just like his throw, he also ran like a girl and screamed like a girl. When he was twenty feet from me, I hopped out of the hole, took aim and hurled a ragged stone straight at his head. Thank God for safety glasses. I cracked the left lens into a dozen sections and he went down as if I'd shot him with a howitzer.

That's about it. When Larry regained consciousness, he staggered to the school nurse, crying all the way. Only one question was asked: "Who threw the rock?"

For me there followed long hours in the principal's office awaiting the eye doctor's verdict on permanent blindness.

"As far as blindness goes," I contemplated telling the principal, "I'm against it."

No, that would never do. Maybe I could raise the money to buy Larry a seeing-eye dog like old man Parker's fat Lab that peed on everyone's leg. Maybe I could donate one of my own eyes. I finally settled on trying to pass for seventeen, joining the Marines, and shipping off to Vietnam as an adviser. Anything, just as long as they didn't make me stay after school for the rest of my life.

In the third grade I'd been unjustly accused of scratching a dirty word onto the wall of the cafeteria. In fact, I'd been playing a childish game of make-believe with a toy car, but the principal didn't fall for the truth and sentenced me to a week of staying after school. I was like a wild animal chained, serving time without end, each tick of the clock like Chinese water torture on my brain.

My transgression was more severe this time and I was now old enough for corporal punishment. For throwing rocks, I got five golf-swing swats from the principal's maple paddle (we called them "licks"). For being a smart-ass ("As far as blindness goes," I told him), I got five more. This from a man who really enjoyed his work. He busted my butt; worse yet, he broke Jewel's heart. She was just down the hall listening to each echoing blow while pretending to teach second graders how to read. Looking back on it, I realize that this was the event that started our move away from San Angelo the following year. Jewel didn't believe in beating children, especially her baby.

I cried softly on five of the swats and howled like a dog on the rest. During the week's enforced vacation that was added on for not telling who else was involved, I played a lot of golf and found that much more enjoyable than sitting on my sore ass.

"THAT LYIN' SUMBITCH!" SAID Beast. "He's got a lot of balls to pull that crap on me."

March's medicine had not set well on the big man's stomach. Not only had Beast's tee shot ended up under an oak tree on number four, but the ball had dropped down so that the trunk of the tree stood between the ball and the spot where Beast should have been standing to make a swing. He could take a left-handed stance and rotate one of his long irons so that the toe of the club pointed straight down at the ground, swing like a southpaw and probably hit it a hundred yards. But hell, March was putting for eagle. Beast had to do more than hack it back into play. He had to pull something out of his hat.

He snatched his one and only fairway wood from out of my hand and began to experiment with various stances: both feet ahead of the tree, both behind it, standing on one foot or the other, and finally bear-hugging the trunk with both arms as if he were humping it. But it was just no use; he couldn't see the ball for the tree.

The best option, at least the one he chose, was to stand with the tree between himself and the green, his body aiming to hit the ball way left, and the face of the three-wood opened to hopefully slice the ball back in the proper direction. He also had to start the ball low to avoid hitting the overhanging oak limbs, *and* he had to stop his follow-through dead or he was likely to carry the club and possibly his hands into the trunk of the tree.

It was cool there in the deep shade, a pleasant spot to watch him consider each of these options as his attention turned step by step from being duped by March to the business at hand.

Taking the club back faster than usual, he tomahawked the ball, carving hard and furious at its upper right corner. Launching out from under the tree like an artillery fusillade, the shot exploded as the clubshaft slammed into the hardwood trunk and snapped cleanly into two pieces.

"Son of a bitch!" Beast screamed as he threw down the short end of the stick. "Son of a bitch never sliced!"

I couldn't believe it. He wasn't cursing about the broken club or the pain that must have vibrated through his hands to his brain. He was pissed off because the ball had failed to do exactly what he wanted, furious because he'd hit it straight when he wanted it to slice.

"Son of a bitch! I should have hit it left-handed!" he said as he stomped off.

The ball's straight flight path had taken it into the woods left of the green—out of bounds. Beast declined to take the penalty stroke and drop another ball beneath the tree, so he was out of the hole—and so was I.

I picked up the two pieces of the three-wood, marveled at the sharp edges of the broken steel, and put them both in the bag.

"Them new shafts break a mite cleaner than the old hickory clubs."

I jerked my head up and saw Roscoe sitting in his cart nearby.

"I used to break a club or two myself, but I got tired of picking them hickory splinters out of my hands so I had to give it up. But like the man said, 'It's better to break one's clubs than to lose one's temper.' "

I had to laugh at that one.

"Now you're laggin' behind, Spud, so quit lollygaggin' around and climb your butt in here."

The passenger's seat was once again empty, Jewel having abandoned Roscoe for a closer look at some wildflowers in the far rough. I thought about telling her to watch for snakes, then remembered that she could handle herself.

"I said haul your butt in here. There's nothing wrong with riding now and then. Hell, I been doing it ever since March blew a hole in my leg."

I looked at him wide-eyed, my face a slow green waiting to be read by an old caddie. I was sure of what he'd said, but unable to believe it.

"Oh yeah, it's true. March was jealous of me and Jewel, so he crippled me with his thirty-ought-six. But never mind that. That's all in the past. Bygones are gone by and all that stuff. Now climb in here and let's have us a chew."

Burying three fingers and a thumb into a pouch of Red Man, Roscoe withdrew a gigantic wad of tobacco and stuffed it into his cud.

"Dig in!" he said, extending the open pouch in my direction.

I looked closer at the jumble of stems and leaves, and the smell about knocked me out of the cart.

"Just pick a cheek and shove it in!" he said. "Jewel tells me you're her blood. I hadn't figgered that. We're gonna be great friends, you and me."

Taking a small pinch, I placed it gingerly into one cheek. It burned like the dickens.

"Hell, boy! We ain't gonna have none of that pussy-style

chewing around here. You ain't got enough to taste. Come on! Make like an outfielder: grab yourself a fistful!"

Aw, what the hell! I crammed my right cheek with the stuff and felt an immediate wave of giddiness.

While we drove slowly to the green, Roscoe began to tell me a little story about golf tempers—his own, that is. Shortly after he and March moved Fowler Oil to Austin, Roscoe goes out by himself for a practice round. But he just can't get it together: one shot a hook, the next a slice. Finally he comes to a dreaded par three, a long shot over water. Fearing the worst, Roscoe takes a big cut at it, and damned if he doesn't hit a nice high shot that soars toward the green. But halfway there a friggin' bird dives at the ball; the two collide and both fall dead in the water. He can't believe it. Of all the damned luck!

Somehow Roscoe avoids losing his temper. Instead—very calmly, according to his reckoning—he decides to quit golf forever. This is not a rash decision. He simply knows it's over. Taking all the balls from his bag, he tosses them down and hits them one at a time into the lake, his only aim a tiny island of pampas grass. His target might as well have been Mars, because each shot is worse than the last: a slice, a duck hook, fat, topped, a shank. Each shot fills him with joy because he's one ball closer to the last damn shot he'll ever have to hit.

"The last ball! Hallelujah, just one more crummy shot," Roscoe told me. "So I take a half-assed swing at the ball . . . and it cuts through the air like a bullet, lands dead in the center of the pampas grass—a virtual hole-in-one! Holy moly! I was stunned. It looked just like the pros! Trying to remember exactly how I did it, I start searching like a madman for a ball, any ball—in the thick grass, in the rough, in the bushes—nothing! Finally, I remember where there's plenty of them balls. So I wade into the pond—damn near drown when my boots fill up with water—and find me a couple of golf balls so I can keep playing.

"You can't quit this game, son!" Roscoe concluded. "It's the game that gets to quit you!"

Either the story or the chew was very moving, for at that moment I hopped out of the cart and upchucked in the flowers by the green.

THESE GUYS REALLY HAD it in for the youth of America. First March offers me a glass of Scotch and a golden opportunity to corrupt my morals, then Roscoe makes a play for my grandmother and forces a wad of tobacco down my throat. Did they want my help, my affection, or my soul? Whatever it was, they sure had a funny way of going about it.

For all I knew, Roscoe's leg could have been the result of childhood polio; I'd seen kids just a few years older than me who had that same kind of limp. Maybe Roscoe was conning me by blaming March. Roscoe had a history of that sort of thing, or so March said. Who was I to believe? Had March entered into a partnership with all of a valuable ranch and left it with half a worthless one? Or had Roscoe come into the deal with two good legs and gone out a cripple? The only answer was that neither was to be trusted: they were both a couple of hustlers.

They used to be partners, not just in the oil business but in golf as well. While March drove me home after that first round, he told me that in the early fifties, when their swings were smooth and the oil business easy, he and Roscoe would travel around Texas laying the sandbaggers' hustle on unsuspecting country clubbers. On the hunt for some winter prey along the Gulf Coast, they'd been set up by the pro at Corpus Christi Country Club with a Mr. Thompson, an out-of-towner who appeared to be an easy mark.

Thompson didn't look anything like a golfer; instead of slacks and a cap, he wore a suit and a gray fedora. March and Roscoe quickly got him into a hundred-dollar Nassau six ways: a hundred on the front nine, two hundred on the back, and three hundred on the total. And Thompson was going to play against March and Roscoe's best ball. It must have seemed like money from home.

Once the bet was set, Mr. Thompson called over a caddie.

"Run out to the black Cadillac," he told the kid, "and fetch my golf clubs for me."

The kid returned empty-handed.

"Did you want the left-handed clubs or the right-handed ones?" the caddie asked.

Mr. Thompson scratched his neck for a minute while he thought.

"Get some of both," he answered. "I need the practice."

"We knew we were screwed," March said. "But we'd have been damned before we'd turn tail and run. I shot 79, Roscoe shot 80, and the man in the fedora took us for four hundred apiece—driving right-handed, chipping from the south, and putting with a two-iron 'cause the caddie forgot to get a putter out of the trunk.

"After the round we found out Mr. Thompson's first name was Ti, as in Titanic Thompson, the king of the cons; and man, he sunk us but good. He took our money and then we all got drunk in the bar and laughed about it. What a grand old scoundrel he was!"

Later, I asked Roscoe if it was true they once played Titanic Thompson, and Roscoe said it was all gospel except for one thing: "March got it backwards as usual: I shot 79 and *March* shot 80."

WHEN MARCH CHIPPED IN for an eagle from just off the fourth green, it no longer mattered that Beast had hit his second shot out of bounds. And Beast could reach the only remaining par five with a driver and a one-iron, so it didn't even matter that he'd broken his three-wood. Nothing mattered except that March bounced his ball into the hole with a little chip shot learned, he said, "from an old Chinaman."

"Well, you can't lose 'em all!" he declared.

"One down with five to go," said Fromholz. "This is getting interesting."

I'd had enough of riding, chewing, and upchucking, so I fell in line with those afoot and started the climb up the hill to the fifth tee. Jewel, siding with the winner again, hopped into March's cart for a ride. Watching this, Roscoe mumbled something that sounded an awful lot like "goddamn her hide," then climbed into his cart and sped off after them.

"This is really getting interesting," said Fromholz.

Now that the sun had burned off the morning dew, we began to suffer under the not-too-pleasant delusion of golfing in a gigantic steam bath. None of us was quite to that point in Texas summer golf where the sun starts burning a hole in your eyes, but it was only a matter of an hour or two.

Needing relief, we lined up at the water well next to the fifth tee. I was last. Jewel, of course, was first.

"William March!" she called out. "You cut out that nonsense and have a cool drink before you keel over dead."

March, in hopes of knocking down a fat pear for his lady love, was tossing a golf club up into the limbs of a big fruit tree that shaded the well. But rather than a pear coming down, his club stayed up, lodged in the branches. Attempting to knock it down, he hung a second club with the first. For a while it looked as though he might lose his whole set to the squirrels, but eventually they all rained down—the clubs, that is. He never did dislodge a pear.

"It's a fine day in Texas," he said. "Blue skies. Gulf breezes. Money on the line!" He turned to me. "A momentous event, Billy. A day you aren't ever going to forget. Lots of big things are gonna happen in your life; you'll have kids. I guess before that you'll probably get married. And if you're lucky, before that you might even get laid!"

I blushed a bright red and Jewel came to my defense.

"William March!" she said. "You be nice to that boy or I'll whip you with an ugly stick!"

"Too late for that," Roscoe snickered.

"Okay! I'm nice. I'm nice. See how nice I am?" March cut in front of Fromholz, filled the long-handled tin cup under the stream of well water, and handed it to me.

"Drink up. A man needs ten glasses of that a day in this sun. Enough to make you sweat. Right, Roscoe?"

"Nobody does it better," Roscoe answered, tilting his bottle for relief and showing us the dark expanding sweat stains that threatened to conquer his entire cowboy shirt.

"Golf is like sex," March said. "You have to take a shower after both."

"I used to think that joke was funny—twenty years ago," said Roscoe.

"It was—then," said March, not the least insulted. "But we got older. And so did the jokes."

"Kid, if it's wisdom you want," Roscoe told me, "I'm your man: never trust a queer or a golfer who wants you to give him strokes."

"Roscoe!" commanded Jewel. "We don't need that kind of talk."

Much to my surprise, Beast came to Jewel's support. "My old man told me to watch out for a guy with the a gimp leg who wants to play for money!"

"Amen to that!" said the guy with the gimp leg. "Watch out for ol' Roscoe; I'll jump on you like ugly on ape!"

"My turn," said Fromholz. "Golf advice," he told me, "ain't worth the wind it's written on. You want to enjoy life like a true bohemian? Get yourself a fat girl: warm in the winter and shady in the summer."

"Very educational," Jewel scolded the whole shameless lot of them. "And oh-so-kind: advising this youngster about the trickeries and meanness of life. Well, here's one for all of you: 'I've lived some years on this planet and I have yet to hear the first syllable of valuable advice from my seniors.' Henry David Thoreau."

They all looked at her, dumbfounded. She was always talking that way, quoting some dead guy that you couldn't remember who he was. I was used to it, but those other guys didn't know whether she was coming or going. Still, they were so taken with her radiant charm and generous smile that they'd have put up with rickets, hives, or the quoting of Scripture just to be near her. Men had been barking up her tree for as long as I could remember, scratching on the screen door like cats in heat, but

Jewel just fended them off with a glass of sun tea and a sprig of fresh mint.

Some women have the knack of capturing men, and others master the fine art of keeping them at bay. Jewel's tools in these conflicting tasks were charm, mystery, and me, which greatly increased my stock with her suitors. Jewel's beaus were always taking me out for milk shakes and burgers or dropping off a wrist-rocket slingshot, a baseball glove, or maybe even some fancy new putter, all in hopes that I'd put in a good word for them.

Even there on the golf course, my relationship to Jewel was increasing my stock to the point that the golfers were beginning to include me almost as a participant in the game. Being the closest to Jewel made me in some ways the most respected of the group.

"Kid, you seem to know a lot about bag shagging," said Roscoe. "Can you play?"

"Can he play?" answered Sandy. "Heck, yes! I've seen him working out on the range, hitting three, four buckets a day, right?"

"Yeah, I guess."

"You guess? Once you beat that slice, you'll be darn good."

I hadn't known Sandy was such a great believer in me.

"Slice, huh?" said Beast. "You'll never be nothing with no slice. I bet you got one of them long, loose, loop-de-loop back-swings with all the power at the top and no finish. I could cure that in a minute. Answer me this, Skinny: How long is the back-swing?"

This had to be a trick question. Nevertheless, I moved my hands from in front of where my belt buckle would have been— if I'd owned a belt—to above and behind my shoulder at the top of my swing.

"That long?" I asked him.

"Just what I figgered. You're all turned around like a dog after his tail."

Beast pulled a club from his bag—only the second time he'd done so all day—and handed it to me. The club felt heavy, but it felt good to grip it like a golfer instead of like a caddie. And it also felt powerful, like I could do no wrong.

"Do it again," he said.

I turned my body and shoulders once more, careful not to take the club back so far.

"Here?"

"Wrong!" He made a little buzzer noise like the ones game shows use when you miss a question. "Wrong, wrong, wrong!"

With everyone watching, this was quickly turning into the most intimidating lesson of my life. Sandy had already helped me with my swing, strengthening my grip and helping me to feel rooted to the ground. He'd also told me about Ben Hogan's "pane of glass" theory concerning swing planes along an axis from the ball through your heart.

"That's the plane the club travels through," Sandy had said. "Actually there's two planes. One going back and a less steep one as you come down to the ball."

That had helped me to get away from my all-arms-no-body swing, but it had, just as Beast guessed, given me a big loop when the clubhead changed direction at the top.

Beast grabbed the club from my hands and set up to hit the ball. "Where's my left shoulder?"

Another trick question. "Right there?"

"Square and level, right?"

I nodded as he took the club to the top of his swing. "Where's my shoulder now?"

"Under your chin."

"Riiiiiight!" He drew the word out over the full length of his takeaway. "So how long is the swing?"

I still didn't know the answer.

"Eight inches—less for a kid. That's the distance the shoulder travels from square to just under your chin. Don't wrap the damn club around you like a vine. Take it back and put it in the slot. Got it?"

"Got it."

I wasn't nearly so sure as I sounded; I just wanted the lesson to be over. But I was not to be so lucky. Advice hung in the air like clothes on a line.

"And don't forget," said Roscoe, taking over the pulpit. "Golf is ninety percent mental, ninety percent skill, and ninety percent luck."

"What's the other thirty percent?" Beast asked in all seriousness.

We did our best not to laugh out loud. Beast was such a good golfer, maybe he didn't need to add past even par.

March had been uncharacteristically quiet through all of this, but he didn't intend to let his archrival get away with being the sage of the group.

"Roscoe," he said, "I always knew you were an unabashed egotist, but I didn't know you were also golf's primary authority."

"Hell, I'm so smart you wouldn't believe it."

"You got that right!"

"Screw you!"

"You been doing that for years, every time I turned my back."

These two couldn't carry on a conversation for ten seconds without coming to an argument. It was hard to believe that they'd put up with each other for so long. This time it was Jewel who came to their rescue.

"Don't you want to see if Mr. Larsen's lesson was functional?"

"Lady," said Beast, "what are you talking about?"

"I think it's time you let Billy hit a ball. You can see if he learned anything."

I protested the best I could: I wasn't warmed up and I didn't have my clubs. But Sandy handed me his driver and offered his shoes.

I looked down at his size nines, still sporting two holes with spots of dried blood from Beast's spikes. I already wore a size twelve; Jewel always said I'd have been seven feet tall if there wasn't so much turned under. Hopping on one foot and then the other, I pulled off my tennies and then, embarrassed by the big holes in the toe of each sock, removed them as well. The grass felt good under my feet.

"Barefoot?" asked Roscoe. "You gonna hit it barefoot?"

"In San Angelo they called him the Wild Indian," Jewel told them.

Everybody had a laugh over that one while March teed up a ball for me. The whole thing was like the customers massaging the masseuse. I gripped the club lightly, stepped up to the ball and closed my left eye into its usual concentrated squint. The rest—as with most good golf shots—was a mystery. The next thing I remember the ball was soaring down the middle of the fairway with a slight draw, then bounding over the ridge out of sight, a near-perfect shot.

There followed an open-mouthed silence.

"How's that?" I asked.

After a beat, they all began talking at once.

"How'd you do that?"

"What were you thinking about?"

"How tight was your grip?"

"See, you put it in the slot . . ."

I did my best to feign nonchalance, but I think they knew.

"Heckuva shot, Billy," said March. "That makes me real proud!"

"Yes Sir!" came a new voice in the group. "That was an admirable endeavor you struck upon there, mister."

Turning our heads in unison, we were surprised to see that our group had grown. From out of nowhere, or so it seemed, a mysterious little man—ninety years old if he was a day—had appeared on the tee.

"A very admirable endeavor, indeed."

I supposed he had walked up the path from the fourth green, but we didn't see him till he was right on us. His clothes were different than any I'd ever seen, Scottish or Chinese or somewhere in between, and I think he wore a beekeeper's helmet on top of his head. The flimsy canvas bag on his shoulder held three or four clubs, one an ancient wood with a hickory shaft. He withdrew the wood from the bag and turned to us with a wrinkly smile.

"Morning," he said. "Mind if I play through?"

We all stood there, dumbfounded. Finally Fromholz took charge.

"All yours, Pops! Hit it good."

The old guy teed up a ball with a Texas tee—meaning he scuffed the sole of the club down into the ground, creating a little peak of turf on which to set his ball. The ball itself was rather yellowed and appeared to be of an entirely different make from anything then in use. He took no practice swing, just stepped up to the ball, took it back effortlessly, made flawless contact and a nice finish. Even with his limited power and antique equipment, the ball flew at least two hundred yards.

"How's that one?" he asked Fromholz, mimicking my own query.

"Solid, Pops! Solid!" replied Fromholz.

"Well, it didn't go far," the old man said with a twinkle. "But I can find it!"

Find it? There was a long narrow indentation *exactly* in the center of the fairway where the ground had sunk along the irrigation pipe. The old man's ball had to come to rest in that depression.

"Thank you, young'uns," he concluded, and before any of us could utter so much as a word of reply, he was gone. I felt as if I were in a trance or something. One minute he was there, and the next he was unshouldering his bag down in the fairway.

"Mother, Mary of Jesus!" said Roscoe. "Did you see that? He split the goalpost! First the kid; now the old geezer. Jewel, you wanna hit one?"

I HAD NOT YET discovered that the basis of life is to be afraid, though Jewel already had me reading my Faulkner, so it was there before me as plain as the nose on my face. But I had not seen it and did not yet know that once I truly accepted fear, I would at last be able to ignore it. And so I walked in the timidity of the young: afraid that Jewel would leave me the way my mother had, afraid of Beast's intimidating demeanor, afraid of the bullies in school who twisted your spine to wring out your tears, afraid to hit the ball from the sand for fear of leaving it there, afraid to do what I knew to be right for fear of being wrong.

But as I bent over in the fifth fairway and picked up the ball that I'd hit there by choking down my fear, a burst of pride welled up in me and I saw for the first time that the track was open, the sky was blue and the way was clear. And I was not the only one to see. March pulled up next to me in his cart and looked me in the eye.

"Like I said on the tee, you make me proud, Billy, real proud."

I did not know why, but I blushed.

"You want some gum?" he asked, holding out a package of Juicy Fruit.

When I reached out to take a piece, he touched my hand.

We'd never even shaken hands before, but I will never forget that he touched me then. He also unwrapped about three sticks of gum for himself, shoved them all in his mouth, and sped away in the cart.

I swung my sock-stuffed tennies over my shoulder and hustled off on my tough bare feet to catch up with Beast. The ball I'd picked up felt warm in my pocket. That was a lucky ball if I ever saw one. And March had put it on a red tee for me too. I wished I'd kept it. A red tee was considered very lucky, but I'd been so excited at the shot that I'd forgotten to pick it up.

Sometimes I wonder if Jewel ever walked in the timidity of the young. For even though she feared Elisha Judson, she refused to let that fear stand in the way of what she felt she must do. Jewel had learned that if there comes a time when the rules or the beliefs that govern your life can be broken then there must follow a time when you learn to no longer need rebellion. That time must come or you are lost. Back in that fateful summer of 1935, it was a full week before Jewel could get a ride from Del Rio back to Sonora. A full week during which her father locked her in her room as punishment for her post–Wing Ding daylight return, a week during which she came to look upon her night of rebellion with great horror. Jewel realized her moments of debauchery hadn't improved her situation at home, or her life in general. And that is the reason, I suspect, that she eventually told me the rest of her story: so that I wouldn't do what she had done.

Jewel's situation was complicated by her sense of fear and honor: fear that her new beau would come howling like a hyena in heat at her father's back door, and honor that it was her duty to get out of the mess she'd gotten herself into. For there could be no doubt that she was not the least bit in love with Rodney or Roger or whatever his name was.

He'd drawn her a crude map to his well site, and she was determined to go there and tell him that what had happened could never happen again. Telling her father she was visiting friends, Jewel embarked on the hot and miserable bus ride from Del Rio to Sonora. The driver let her off where a bald rubber truck tire hung in a tree to mark the faint sidetrack into rough country. As the bus rumbled away, she picked her way down the packed caliche road, presumably toward the well.

Topping the ridge of a hill, her handbag hanging limply at her side, she halted, wide-eyed with wonder at the noisy clanging of the salvaged and borrowed drilling rig that whip-snaked a rusted cable through a protesting crownblock and down into the violated ground. The crooked drilling tower was lashed and welded together from mismatched timbers and steel scavenged from broken-down tractors and wrecked trucks and stolen from other wells. Cowering beneath it was a wood-fired boiler that was patched and rusted and patched again, hissing and belching like a giant snake about to explode from inhaling too many rats.

It put her in mind of her father, who often preached that oil was the God-given source of fire and brimstone and was used to fuel the furnaces of Hades. If those damned oilmen didn't cease the withdrawal of the oil from the earth, they might cause the fires to go out. In his eyes they were evil, wicked men, extinguishing the all-important threat of eternal damnation.

Two small, dark-skinned Mexican men, who looked in no way evil, were chopping and tossing cedar stumps into the boiler fire. What's-his-name was nowhere in sight, and neither was the dusty red pickup in which she'd made her bed.

"¿Dónde está Señor Roger?" she asked the Mexicans, yelling over the noise.

"*¿Cómo?*" they replied.

"*¿Señor Roger? ¿Dónde está?*"

"*¡Lo siento! ¡No hablo Español¡*" one of them answered, flashing pearly teeth studded with a variety of metal and stone fillings.

Having had their joke, they directed her to another man as he stepped clear of the crownblock atop the drilling platform. Spotlessly clean amid the all-pervading grime, he was studying the copper-colored tailings that streamed out of the hole. When his men yelled to him, he turned to see a stunning mirage in a long dress and sun hat. Dropping a heavy wrench on his own toe, he limped and climbed and leapt down to greet her.

Beneath his clean clothes he was tan to the bone and his eyes shone brightly through the sweat that beaded on his forehead. He came over and extended a hand that was hot to her touch. As she shook the hand and looked into his bright, clear eyes she fell instantly and madly in love with him. His name, I know now, was William March.

"GET *OWN* UP THERE!" said March as his ball flew a hundred and fifty yards down the fairway and bounded up the slope in front of the fifth green.

Not that I'd noticed at the time how he pronounced words like "on." It wasn't until years later, after I'd spent some time out of the state, that I realized how funny and wonderful we Texans talk. The lazy combination of two words into one (Sa-nangelo), three words into two ("Haw yew?") and the even lazier tongue that turns "fine" into "fahn," all require a more removed perspective before they really come home to roost. It's like eating a chicken-fried steak all smothered in cream gravy—you really have to miss it awhile before you begin to appreciate it properly.

"Fahn-lookin' shot, March!" said Roscoe, outdoing March's accent by a power of five. "Ah bulieve wur both puttin'."

"You are right as rain!" replied March. Their tee shots had been side by side in the fifth fairway and, incredibly, their second shots were nearly kissing on the green.

"Hot damn, this is almost fun!" said Roscoe.

"Just like old times," said March. "You know, it's not too late to shake hands, pool our cash, and go someplace godforsaken to drill a well."

Roscoe looked him up and down in amazement. "Sun getting to you, March?"

"Nah! Don't you remember when we stood together and took on all comers, butt to butt against the sunrise and the sunset, so those other bastards always had the glare in their eyes?"

March grabbed the bottle from Roscoe. "Here's to us; to hell with them!"

Then came the most unimaginable occurrence of the day: Roscoe's perpetual frown relaxed for a moment; his squinty eyes opened just wide enough so we could see they were brown; his tight, cracked lips separated a bit; and, ever so slowly, some fond memory came blooming across his face like a rose. It almost made you want to smell him; the sheer epiphany of some forgotten adventure long since misplaced in that attic full of mostly rotting memories of their mutual past. It only lasted a few moments, then Roscoe's mind began to wander into darker corners. The blazing rose just shriveled back into the same old grouchy curmudgeon who chewed and spit and scratched his ass, and had long since forgotten that life could be basically good with just a bit of shit thrown in rather than the other way around.

Roscoe snatched the bottle back from March.

"And all I got to do to make us unbeatable again is just stick out my hand and say the word, right?"

"Yeah," said March, extending his open hand. "Why not?"

"Aw hell, March!" said Roscoe. "That's a bunch of crap if I ever heard any! We ain't been friends for thirty years, not since the moment we both set eyes on Miss Jewel Anne Hemphill there. I got her. You wanted her; then you got her. Then she didn't want you anymore and I got her back."

Through all of this talk, Jewel had stood quietly to one side, weaving the wildflowers she had picked into the sun hat which she often carried in her bag. Now she placed the hat on her head and stepped between the two men. "Nobody's got me now," she said.

"That's true enough," said Roscoe. "But March and I aim to change that, don't we, March? And that's why we ain't calling off nothing: a bet's a bet. Play ball!"

It looked like the good part was over, so I hustled along to catch up with Beast. My tennies bounced and swung from my shoulder as I stretched out my strides in the direction of the left rough where my boss was stomping around looking for his ball. Always trying to get that extra edge, Beast had actually tried to drive the green by bounding one down the road that paralleled the fairway. I guess the ball must have taken an asphalt hop in the wrong direction because it was nowhere in sight. But before I could get to him, Beast began raving like a madman.

"Aigghhhhh!" he screamed. It was an awkward shriek, like he hadn't had much opportunity to express fear.

I ran toward him; with each step the big bag bounced off my shoulder and slammed down on my hip, while the flopping tennies kicked me double-time in the back and chest. I tried to find some kind of smooth canter, but both bag and the tennies continued to rattle my bones.

"Yeee-aigghhhh!" hollered Beast again. His screams were improving with practice and had now attracted everyone's attention. March and Roscoe were driving over in their carts, but I was the closest, about twenty feet from him when he finally got out an intelligible word.

"S-s-snake!" he hollered as if it were biting him in his private parts. "S-s-snake!"

Hearing the reference to slithering reptiles stopped me in my tracks. There was no use carrying this Wild Indian thing too far. I unslung my tennies from the bag, and by the time the others arrived, I had the shoes on my feet.

March, Roscoe and I walked up together and, sure enough, we found Beast darn near cornered by a snake—a diamond-back rattler, to be precise. We couldn't tell how long the snake was because it was coiled around Beast's ball as if it were hatching an egg. Beast's behind side was backed up against a barbed-wire fence, and as he moved to get away, the snake pulled back its head in indication of striking at him.

"Somebody kill it," begged Beast. "Please somebody kill it!"

"Ease on out of there, son," advised March. "Nice and slow-like."

"I cain't. My pants are hung on the bob wire. You gotta kill it."

Roscoe strolled closer, nonchalant. "Well, I've seen a snake-milking, a toad-roping, and a duck fart under water," he said. "But I'll be damned if this chicken squawking don't beat all!" He turned back to March like he'd discovered something marvelous. "I think the big man's afraid of snakes!"

"Hell, yes, I'm afraid of snakes!" Beast whimpered. "Somebody kill it."

"Calm down, big guy," said Roscoe. "No reason to panic. You get a free drop, right Fromholz?"

By this time Fromholz, Sandy and even Jewel had arrived to survey the situation. Fromholz stepped in next to Roscoe, about six feet from the snake and just out of striking range.

"A drop? For a rattlebug?" said Fromholz. "Not a chance. A snake is a natural hazard."

"Aw, hell, of course he gets a drop!" argued Roscoe. "You look in that dang rule book! There's gotta be something in there about snakes!"

"Forget the damn drop and kill the snake!" pleaded Beast.

"Hell, no, we won't forget the drop! We ain't counting you

out of the hole, pawd-no!" Roscoe turned back to Fromholz. "Ref, this just ain't fair!"

"Maybe not, but that's my ruling," said Fromholz.

"I don't believe this!" said Beast. "I'm about to get eat up by a snake and you guys are arguing *rules*!"

The three of them would have bickered over that rattler till they were blue in the face if one sane voice hadn't risen calmly above the din.

"Give *me* a golf stick."

We all turned slowly to look at Jewel, who was holding out her hand for a weapon.

"Give me a club," she repeated. "I'll kill it."

I was about five years old. Jewel was showing me the ruins of the Mission San Saba, an eighteenth-century Spanish outpost on the San Saba River that lasted a dozen years before the Indians drove the heathen Catholics back to the coast.

Walking a few feet ahead of her, I was about to climb the stone steps into one of the roofless buildings when Jewel told me to freeze. I'd never heard her speak with such a chill and it frightened me bad. I froze in my tracks and stayed there.

There was a snake, she said, a rattlesnake, coiled just in front of me. I couldn't see it; my eyes were darting all around in search of the snake, but all I could focus on was Jewel's hand edging ever so slowly toward a heavy oak log in the dry leaves. She steadily closed the gap till at long last she had her flattened palm against the log, and then her fingers around it. Just as slowly, that thick timber came up into the air, rising above my head, and exactly as it crashed down from the sky like an instrument of God, I saw the snake, coiled on a little stone ledge not eighteen inches from my face with its cold eyes fixed on mine. The snake struck forward and a hand's width from my eyes, the log came down squarely on its head. I jumped back, and Jewel screamed as she pounded that snake's head over and over and over until it almost became a part of the stone path.

"You son of a bitch!" Jewel screamed through her tears as she continued to swing the log. "You son of a bitch! You leave my baby alone!"

She just kept pounding and screaming and crying until finally I had to wrap my arms around her leg and tell her the snake was dead.

"Jewel!" warned Roscoe. "You stay back!"

"Yeah," said Beast. "Skinny, you kill it."

"Billy?" said Fromholz in disgust. "Why, you pantywaist!"

Having heard all he cared to hear, Fromholz reached into the pocket of his jacket—actually I think he reached right *through* the pocket of the jacket. From somewhere beneath it he withdrew a large six-shooting pistola and nonchalantly blasted that snake's head off with one loud, terrifying shot. Then with a second shot he blew off its rattle. We all jumped when the gun went off, but none higher than Beast who leapt straight into the air, tearing his pants on the fence.

"Souvenir for you, kid," said Fromholz, pointing to the still-quivering rattle.

I picked it up gently. The rattle twitched on my palm as I counted the sections—eleven of them—one for each skin the snake had shed during its life. I collected stuff like that: little things that meant something to me. They were all at home in an old wooden cigar box with a warped top that wouldn't close: arrowheads and flint scrapers, old-timey marbles made of clay, two stamps from Tanzania showing gigantic white birds in flight, and even a harmonica with *Herb Shriner's Harmonicats* engraved on it. But this rattle was the best of all.

"Six-iron always was my best club," said Fromholz, putting the pistol away as quickly as he'd produced it.

"Damn! I ripped my pants!" complained Beast.

"That ain't so bad," answered Roscoe. "We thought you was going to wet 'em! Now have a shot."

The others backed away from the messy snake while I selected a seven-iron and handed it to Beast. He didn't even look to see what club it was. As he addressed the ball, I could see his hands quivering like the snake's rattle. After a long time of just standing there, he backed away and called to Roscoe.

"What the hell is that guy doing with a gun?" he whispered in a shrill voice.

"Protecting you, evidently. What's the problem?" said Roscoe.

"He's not protecting me!" said Beast in a panic. "He's here to get me. I owe Binion a lot of money. If we lose, that guy's gonna kill me, ain't he?"

Roscoe didn't answer.

"Ain't he?" repeated Beast. "Ain't he gonna kill me if we lose?"

Roscoe pursed his lips together and rubbed his tongue around the inside of his mouth. Either he'd lost his chew or he was searching for something to say. Finally it came to him.

"Don't lose."

WHEN THE MONEY'S ON the line, golf becomes like poker: you can play to win or you can play to not lose. Or, if you don't have any real idea what the difference is, you can do what most golfers *and* poker players do: play to lose. They don't know that's what they're doing, but the loss is just as inevitable as if they had drawn four cards to a deuce kicker or used a putter off the tee.

Shortly after buying that first five-iron at Santa Fe Park, I learned that golf is much harder than it looks. So after a lot of frustration and a good deal of pleading, Jewel finally enrolled me in a junior golf class.

I was by far the youngest student in the class. The course covered everything from driving to irons, chipping to putting, and even included a little lecture about common courtesy. It was complete in every way except one: the coach hardly touched on the rules. Oh sure, they told us about a number of penalties: stroke and distance for out of bounds, two strokes for hitting the pin when putting, and a whole variety of strokes for encountering water, lateral or otherwise. All examples of how the rules worked against us, but nothing about how the rules might work *for* us. They told us what to do if you lost a ball, but they never told us anything about what to do if you found a ball, but couldn't figure out how to hit it. And on the very first hole of the class graduation tournament, that was exactly what my drive rolled into: an unplayable lie.

It was Bermuda grass, about eighteen inches deep. For most kids the ball would have been lost, but I knew it was in there. My eyes did not deceive. And when I found it nestled at the bottom of that jungle, I knew right away that I could never hit it out. But I'd never heard of an unplayable lie, that I could just take a one-stroke penalty and drop the ball out within two club lengths. I pulled out a seven-iron—having already graduated to a larger mismatched set of clubs—and I began to whale away.

Two, three, four; hit it some more. Five and six; change sticks. Seven, eight, nine; let out a little whine. Ten, eleven; bad-mouth heaven.

By fifteen the ball still hadn't moved, but I was digging a nice tunnel toward it. How high can an eight-year-old count anyway?

I got the ball out of that patch of grass on the twenty-second stroke. Then a kid who was a couple of years older than me came over laughing and told me I could have dropped it out with one penalty stroke. I stood on my tiptoes and punched him in the nose.

My final score was one hundred and thirty-eight, for which they gave me a trophy in the shape of a boxer for fighting the course (not to mention the other golfers). Just like Sandy's consolation trophy when Beast was disqualified for gambling, I refused to accept it. A trophy is for the winner. The awfully adult lesson I learned is that it's often not that important if you win, only that you don't finish last.

My third-grade pals and I used to tell a riddle about a two-man Olympic race won by an American (of course) and lost by a Russian. The headline in Russia read: RUSSIAN SECOND. AMERICAN NEXT TO LAST.

*   *   *

Unfortunately, Sandy and March still seemed more likely to come in second than next to last. After Roscoe's admonition about not losing, Beast hit his shot from next to a headless-but-still-squirming snake to the front of the fifth green. I tended the pin while he stalked the putt for the kill. He studied it from all sides, plumb-bobbing it from back and front, then bent over it with the usual cigarette dangling from his mouth.

"Don't be short," warned Roscoe as Beast was about to putt. Beast tilted his head menacingly in Roscoe's direction, then looked back down at the ball and stroked it hard up the slope.

I was surprised how fast it was coming at me. Hurriedly I pulled on the pin. Nothing happened. Confused, I pulled again: still nothing. The pin was stuck in the cup.

"Pull it!" yelled Beast.

I pulled harder. Nothing.

"Pull it!" hollered Beast and Roscoe.

At the last second I yanked hard, dragging both pin and metal cup up out of the hole. It happened so fast I didn't even know I'd done it. The ball barreled straight at what should have been a hole, struck the raised cup, and bounced about three feet away.

With the pin and cup still in my hand, I looked up in horror and saw Beast charging at me. His putter was cocked back behind his head like a baseball bat, and a scream of rage was issuing from his mouth. It didn't occur to me to run. After all, I was guilty. I had pulled the cup up. I had kept him from winning the same hole on which he'd nearly been killed by a snake. Whatever he did to me—and it looked as if he was going to lop my head off—was certainly my due.

About ten feet of the charge and two seconds of my life remained when Fromholz stuck out a foot at the same time that he cuffed Beast on the back of the neck with the six-shooter. An elephant gun wouldn't have brought the big man down any faster.

While Beast was coming to his senses, Fromholz proceeded to investigate the stuck pin and quickly discovered that someone had put chewing gum in the bottom of the cup. Chewing gum? I quickly swallowed mine and glanced over to March. He no longer seemed to be chewing his, either.

That's twice, I thought. That's twice he cheated.

Beast was learning some hard lessons. His three-wood was broken, his pants were torn, and there was a knot on his head about the size of one of the smaller British golf balls. On top of that, the putt was not considered good.

Fromholz kindly waived the penalty for striking the pin with a putt from on the green because, technically, the ball had struck the cup. But the ball was not in the hole and the birdie had flown the coop. With Fromholz's help I separated the pin from the cup, and replaced the latter in its hole so the others could putt. But still no birdie putts went in, and number five was halved by pars from both teams.

"No blood," said Fromholz. "Well, not much anyways. Four holes to go, gentlemen. Fowler and Larsen are still one up."

"Not for long," said March with a grin. "Not for long."

THE BUMP ON HIS noggin was sufficient to deter Beast from beheading me, but it didn't keep him from methodically yanking open each of the ten or twelve zippers on his bag, turning it upside down, and dumping the clubs, balls, tees, cigarettes, matches, and miscellaneous junk in a pile on the fringe of the green.

"Pick 'em up!" he ordered; then stomped off cursing. "What the hell kind of crummy course is this? Bunch of damn cheap greens!"

I gathered up the mess, trying to remember whether the extra shoe spikes went in the pocket with the tees, and if the divot-repair and club-cleaning tools had a place of their own. At the same time I was feeling guilty for what I'd done, and inwardly, I guess, I was blaming March, who must have been the cause of it all.

Twice now he'd cheated, and that was only what I knew about. Who knew, maybe March had put that snake by Beast's ball. And even if that theory was a little far-fetched, I also suspected that he had something to do with the weird cutting of the greens, which continued to be alternately slow and fast.

And then I noticed that March was standing there by my side. Whether he'd come to apologize, bribe me, or beg my forgiveness, I didn't know. He removed his hat—a straw version of LBJ's Open Road Stetson—and wiped the sweat from his brow. I realized that now was the time to come clean and confront him. But as I opened my mouth to speak, his words came first.

"Found something you might take an interest in, young'un."

He held out his closed hand and unwrapped his leathery fingers to reveal an ugly rock just a little smaller than a golf ball. It was a burnt reddish-brown color and it appeared to be both exploded like a kernel of popcorn and melted around the edges.

"Take it."

He dropped the rock in my hand in the same manner as the stick of gum. I was astonished at its weight. It seemed more like lead than a rock.

"I figgered a guy that keeps a snake rattle in his pocket needs some good ju-ju to go with it. And that's what you got there: ju-ju, magic, good vibes, as Fromholz would say."

I didn't know what he was talking about.

"It's a meteorite," he told me. "A moon rock. I found it back there in the rough. Must've been a giant meteor hit here hundreds of years ago. We're probably standing in the crater."

I looked around at the large bowl depression surrounding us and the green.

"Yeah?"

"Moon rocks are magic, you know. You hold 'em tight in your hand and concentrate heart and soul on what you want."

He had to be pulling my leg.

"You mean I wish for a Frito pie or to get out of doing my homework?" I asked him skeptically.

"No! That ain't it at all! Nothing selfish. Moon rocks are very perceptive. They know the difference between a grabby little piss-ant and someone in true need. You think magic is about a Frito pie, son? No, sir! Magic is the most basic form of nature.

You wanna learn something in life, you hang on to that moon rock and you think for a while about what it takes to make a miracle."

I looked down at the heavy pellet in my hand. A major interest in seventh-grade science told me it had probably been snatched from a passing asteroid cloud by the earth's gravity. Most likely it was comprised primarily of nickel and iron that had been melted when speeding through our atmosphere. Once on earth it had remained undisturbed until March found it and handed it to me with this far-fetched tale that only a kid would believe. And yet I did believe it. I believed it because he'd given me something special, because I was a kid who wanted to believe. Because he'd made it magic. My magic.

March patted me on the head and left me to finish my cleanup. It wasn't till I put the rock in my pocket that I realized I'd forgotten to confront him about cheating.

Beast's bag finally reassembled, I caught up with Jewel and we walked up to the sixth tee. She saw the worried look on my face and told me not to feel bad about yanking up the cup.

"If one person was cheating," I asked her, "and another person knew it, should he rat on them? I mean, are you cheating too if you know about it and you don't tell? Or are you just a snitch if you do tell?"

"Hypothetically?" Jewel asked me.

"Oh, yes ma'am!" I told her. "Hypothetically. Definitely."

We walked on a ways to the shade beneath a large cluster of live oaks, our feet rustling through the small brown leaves of years past. In the top of the trees two cicadas buzzed back and forth to each other.

"No. I don't think you should tell," she said. "Hypothetically or otherwise."

"Why not?"

She didn't answer at first, so I gathered my courage and took the plunge into the great unknown.

"Just because March is my grandfather?" I asked her.

I shifted the bag higher onto my shoulder and the cicadas grew silent.

"No. Not because of that."

I bit softly on my lip. Here was final confirmation of what I had suspected since Jewel first sent me to caddie for him weeks ago.

"Not just because March is your grandfather, but also because I'm in love with him. Because I've always been in love with him. And because he needs to win. You're asking about something being right and something being wrong, Billy. Well you look in those two men's eyes, then you tell me who is right and who is wrong."

23

AFTER ALL THIS TIME, it's hard for me to separate what I knew then about Jewel's early time with March and Roscoe from what I learned in the time that followed that amazing day. During my junior and senior high school years, Jewel would sometimes get a faraway look in her eyes, and the corners of her mouth would crawl slowly upward. I knew that meant she was going to tell me about some picnic with March on the Dry Devil's River, or of the letters she'd written that he'd never answered. The odd part was that she never seemed bitter to have lost those thirty years with the man she fell in love with that day at the well.

Since Jewel had come all the way from Del Rio with the honorable intention of letting Roscoe down easy, she managed to convince herself that suddenly falling in love with March was not a problem. Roscoe had been off fetching the mail and supplies when she arrived, so she didn't actually have the opportunity to tell him the original purpose of her visit. Surely the right time and place would present itself, she thought. Unfortunately, the right time and place never arrived.

March and Jewel became fast friends and soon-to-be lovers. Because of what had already transpired between Jewel and Roscoe, neither of them was immediately eager to take the ultimate step of intimacy. A true courtship ensued. Traveling to Del Rio as often as he could get away from the well, March would formally request the honor of Jewel's company from her father the preacher. That Elisha Judson would grant this permission indicates just what a smooth talker March must have been.

There being little or no nightlife in Del Rio, March and Jewel would head across the river for dinner and dancing in the festive town of Villa Acuña, Mexico. Their favorite place was Ma Crosby's, where they ate fried catfish fresh from the Rio Grande, washing it down with ice-cold Carta Blancas drunk from small, often-refilled glasses barely four inches high. The idea was that the beer go down fast and cold and easy.

There were *cantadas* and *bailles* under the stars in the main plaza and numerous *bandidos* of Pancho Villa's former employ singing ballads and telling heroic tales of the Mexican Revolution. To appease Roscoe—and because he was more fun back then than later in his life—they sometimes invited him to come along.

Jewel gave little thought to Roscoe's feelings in all this. It wasn't as though he had been in love with her, or as if they'd spent five sober minutes together. But March knew better. He'd seen another side of Roscoe and he knew that it was only a matter of time before his partner's jealousy erupted in a violent rage, much like the well they were still hoping to bring in any day.

After two months of this uncomfortable situation, March left one night without telling Roscoe. Driving down to Del Rio in the very same truck in which Jewel had forever misplaced her virginity, March found Jewel waiting for him across the street from her father's Victorian mansion.

They drove slowly over the rickety bridge that barely spanned the muddy Rio Grande, and waved at a new friend who guarded the international border from a comfortable seated position, leaning way back on two legs of his chair. After convincing a local merchant to reopen her dress shop, they strolled arm in arm to Villa Acuña's main cathedral. There—in the presence of a priest, a nun and a half-wit—they were married.

"For long as you both should live," pronounced the priest in his broken English.

It was the first time either of them had been in a Catholic church.

Their honeymoon took them all the way back to Sonora, where they spread a blanket beneath the brilliant night sky on a point of land that would in three years become the ninth tee of a strange new sporting field, but which that night was a vantage point to a whole new universe.

Imagining them when they were young, it was easy for me to picture how March and Jewel would have lain together, would have rolled and tossed among the thick woolen blankets, Jewel grasping at tightened muscles, and March with fistfuls of hair, both sighing at the joy and wincing at the pain of being in love. Neither would have the slightest idea that the son of the daughter they begot that night would only be able to compare their tryst with a night he spent forty years later atop a building in Paris with a girl who knew just three words of English.

The red wine and baguettes that kept that beautiful French girl and myself going till dawn tasted to me like the warm beer and cold tacos that March and Jewel bought from a vendor in Mexico and carried to their wedding supper on the hill. My gaze wandered over the city of lights and I thought of the meteor shower Jewel told me they saw that night. The honking of Parisian horns became the hooting of owls, and whatever type of creatures were scurrying about, be they rats or cats, were to me a kit of young foxes come to bask in the glory of the night, to roll and tumble together in scratching, nipping, biting yelps of pain and innocence.

As we awakened with the coming dawn, perhaps like March before me, I wondered if we had conceived a child. To this day I wonder still, because I never saw her again.

THERE WAS A LITTLE outhouse in the middle of the golf course, and from the sixth tee we could all hear Beast in there exercising his temper and his golf shoes on the sheet-metal walls and wooden throne.

"Whooo-eee!" said Roscoe. "Glad he's not mad at me!"

Sandy was swinging his driver to stay loose, and Fromholz just sat still and watched us all, buzzardlike, from his perch on the stump of an old rotted fruit tree. If someone were to fall over dead, I thought, it wouldn't take him long to hop over and peck out one of our eyes to match his own.

Jewel and March stood close to each other at one side of the tee. Jewel was speaking softly to him. I couldn't hear her words, but March's sad blue eyes were staring in my direction all the while.

When she'd had her say, March came walking over toward me. Again he held out his closed hand as if to give me something, but when he uncurled the fingers, there was no chewing gum or moon rock. This time there was only an open hand reaching out to me. It was my turn to put something in his hand. I extended my arm and opened my clenched fingers slowly and we shook hands until a tear appeared in the corner of March's eye and rolled slowly down his cheek.

"Jewel tells me you're a good boy," he said.

"She thinks so."

"Well, Jewel's an excellent judge of character," he said. "Except in Roscoe's case . . . and mine. I guess there's no denying that I let her down sadly. I hope that hasn't cursed me forever. I'm not a bad guy. I've always tried to get some enjoyment out of life. I try to take care of my business and my friends. Now I'm trying to take care of my family."

I gave him a weak smile.

"I feel bad when I make the wrong decisions," he continued. "And I forget to notice when I make the right ones. I don't hit a guy when he's down. And I'm just beginning to learn that when somebody knocks me down, I'm gonna get right back up again. I been down on my knees a long time, but never again. However long I got left, I'd like to spend it with my head held high. I'd like for you to be proud of me. I'd like for the two of us to be friends. And I wish I had a little more time. There's a lot of places and things I'd like to show you."

"I'd like to see 'em all," I told him, fighting back a tear of my own.

"Someday, everything I own'll belong to you. My daddy's ranch will be your ranch, my golf course yours too. It's a beautiful land. My heart left with Jewel, but my soul is out there on that unforgiving land."

The *Llano Estacado*—"staked plains" it means in Spanish. Supposedly the conquistadors marked their way across the Indian country with stakes so as to find their way back to the gulf, laden with the gold of seven cities. But secretly they expected death at every turn, and believed that their souls—lost angels—would need the stakes to guide them back to a civilized afterlife. Then, as they traveled farther into the country, their actions grew more and more barbarous and they thought less and less of becoming angels.

From the estuaries and intercoastal tide pools of the gulf, there's no way to tell just how God-almighty big or how unbelievably dry this land can be. The early settlers, from the Spanish all the way through March's Irish ancestors, entered this vast scape through the mouths of its rivers—rivers that run neither wide like the Mississippi nor deep like the Columbia.

Instead, numerous small rivers meander back through the sunken coastal plains to their time-eroded cuts of the elevated Balcones Fault and beyond into the hostile canyons, draws and creeks where ancient man made his home. That habitation of thousands of years is still given witness by stacked-rock burial mounds, spent or discarded tools of work and war, and limestone cliffs painted in the glyphs of their written language.

If, like the original inhabitants, you continue to follow the water to its source, you'll eventually find a limestone crevice, grown all around in ferns and sweet watercress, with a freshet of cold spring water gushing out, gathering with other trickles and founts and warming slowly as it heads to the sea. But if you follow the riverbeds farther inland, beyond the springs, you'll find the isolated pools that remain from the last rain and river rise; the catfish trapped in ever-dwindling puddles as they flounder in panic until raccoons or bobcats feast on their flesh and drink the last of the water. Only bleached skeletons remain on the baked and cracked soil which cries out for rain farther upstream.

And still the canyons continue on, past any signs of water but their own eroded existence, cutting into country that survives by hoarding more, by needing less. The prickly pear cactus, fat even through the drought until the cattle or the buffalo, dying for water, eat them thorns and all. The mesquite trees, with tiny leaves catching little of the hot sun and providing minimal shade; the thin-bladed grass growing lush in the violent spring storms and waiting patiently, brown but standing tall, through the passing of the other seasons. The wildflowers springing forth in brilliant rainbows after the storm, then burning brown till their seedpods explode, scattering future life to the southwest winds. The snakes, the lizards and the horny toads, all living as can on gathered dew and, like the larger animals, keeping one eye cocked to the sky and one ear to the ground for the hopeful sound of distant thunder.

And then there is man, greediest of consumers: grudgingly adapting through conservation, then lowered expectations, and lastly by insanity. Postponing the inevitable by digging wells or drilling, by constructing dams to hoard in times of plenty, by defending their impoundments against the downstream thirsty with ancient yellowed papers, bribes or guns. By hiring charlatans: white-whiskered old men, crazy Indians, fireworks experts, aviators, scientists, and quacks of all denomination; each promising to make it rain, each coming on the happy rumor of success and leaving on the sad fact of failure.

All that continues unchanged is the vastness of the land and the smallness of man; never conquering but sometimes adapting; looking alternately reddened and browned, increasingly cracked and tanned like a discarded hide, becoming in apparition more and more like an organ or appendage of the living land; and ending up as dust, blowing on the hot breeze, sighing contentedly at the sound of soothing thunder, waiting like all the land for the rain to come, waiting to be washed back to the distant sea.

These were all things I learned and confirmed in the years after I met William March, but I first saw them in his lined eyes and felt them in his calloused hand as it dawned upon me that, if Jewel had become my mother, then he had become what I had never had, and always wanted, a father.

March and I sat down on the grassy slope next to the sixth tee, leaned back on our elbows, and looked up at the sky. The wind had begun to blow hot like a furnace, a sure sign that summer was here to stay. The sun blazed down, an ill-defined orb suspended in a perfect pale-blue bowl that had been inverted dead center on top of our group. How curious that no matter where you stand on earth, your single-point perspective testifies that you are the center of the universe.

I started to speak. I wanted to ask him what was going to happen to us, but March shushed me into quiet attention. After a short silence I began to hear what he heard: bees searching out a blossom, a woodpecker hard at work, the wind rustling the cedars that lined the course, and way off in the distance, a truck whining up a big hill on the Llano highway, then shifting into a lower gear.

A funny bird with two long, skinny tail feathers flapped and glided over our heads, then flapped and glided again. Dipping and twisting his auburn-colored tail feathers gracefully like a rudder, the bird steered itself away from our upturned gaze.

"Scissortail!" said March softly. "That's my favorite bird!"

I thought he'd said the same thing about a mockingbird that had pestered the group earlier, and I imagined that he probably said it about all of them.

"You got a girlfriend at that new school of yours?" he asked.

"No Sir," I lied.

"Well, treat her good, son. You won't regret it."

WHEN WE MOVED FROM San Angelo, Jewel had just sent her twenty-third class of students on to the third grade, and I had moved to the eighth. Since I'd started school a year younger than the other kids of my grade, I'd long lagged behind my pals in ability at contact sports and interest in girls, so I really hadn't bothered with either.

When we arrived in Austin I discovered, to my absolute horror, that school was still in session. Jewel, always the teacher, insisted that I finish out the term in my new school, essentially graduating from the seventh grade all over again.

"Haven't you heard of double indemnity?" I asked her.

But Jewel's natural wisdom was at work in its usual wondrous way. Rather than spending a friendless summer in a new town, I had a little time to get acquainted. And my best consolation turned out to be that the end-of-school dance had not yet been held. Much to my surprise, I was asked by a girl to be her date. She was completing the ninth grade but she invited me to be her escort because, unlike the boys her age, we saw eye-to-eye. After all, I was descended from Adoniram, Lord of Height.

Jewel drove us to the dance while I nervously tried to pin a gigantic corsage to a slender shoulder strap on my date's dress—about as humiliating an experience as a young teen is gonna find.

The similarities to Jewel's Wing Ding were few. The kids were seventh-to-ninth graders, and the copy band played 1965's rock-n-roll favorites, including what seemed like an awful lot of slow tunes, during each of which my date held me closer and tighter while my body temperature rose about five degrees per song.

The funny thing is I don't even remember her name. But I'll never forget that while we danced close—cheek to cheek, pelvis to pelvis—every time her hip swayed out to the right it gave a little bouncing pop as it shifted in the other direction.

Curious to discover whether this was some sexual secret about which I knew nothing or whether she merely had an artificial hip in need of lubrication, I just kept pushing her hip out there with my own. I pushed and we swayed and my date popped in time to the music until, soaked to the skin, I danced us over to the refreshment table. We drank three quick, cold glasses of punch, not knowing that it had been spiked by some smart aleck with 180-proof Everclear. Outside the gym we gleefully and groggily leaned against each other face-to-face. Our lips touched and she so completely surprised me when she slipped her tongue into my mouth that I must've jumped three feet into the air.

When summer was over she'd be moving up to high school where all the boys were tall. So I knew I only had three months to figure out some way to make it happen again. As it turned out, March's advice to treat her good was perhaps the single greatest pearl of wisdom I would ever be given.

"Are you gonna marry Jewel?" I asked March.

"Far as I know, we are married," he told me. "It's been a long time, but I haven't heard any mention of divorce."

"I mean, are you gonna live with her like you were married?"

March laughed. "I don't rightly know, son. I been single most of my life, just staying out late and hanging around with my bad habits. Fear and whiskey kept me going. I haven't run out of whiskey yet, but I about used up my ration of fear. What I'm trying to say is, it's up to Jewel. And you, of course. It's up to you and Jewel."

He gave me a smile and I smiled right back at him. The bees were still humming sweetly and I laid back on the cool grass and closed my eyes for a few seconds to think about how my new life was going to be: French-kissing with older girls, going fishing with my dad March, and playing golf with Sandy until it was too dark to find your ball.

The next thing I remember a shadow came across the face of the sun. I opened my sleepy eyes and blinked up at a gigantic figure.

"Skinny, get up off your bony ass and hand me my driver!"

I scrambled to my feet, noticing that March was already back at his cart.

"Billy!" I said to Beast. "My name is *Billy*!"

While I had napped, Sandy had evidently stayed loose by swinging his driver to and fro. I looked into his blue eyes and saw that he'd found some kind of electric golf groove. It was funny about Sandy's eyes. They changed color with the sky and his emotions; clear blue now, where earlier they had been hazy and gray with the morning overcast. At night they deepened to a dark royal blue, and if you sneaked a close enough look, you could almost see the stars in the little flecks of his irises. In San Angelo he once hit his number ten tee shot into the murky South Concho River. I'd never seen him lose his temper and I felt sure this would be the time, but it only affected his eyes, which assumed the musty hazel color of the water until we left the hole and the river well behind with an eagle on the par-five eleventh.

Along with his fair-haired fraternity-boy good looks, those mysterious eyes made Sandy a bull's-eye target for women wherever he went. But he didn't even seem to notice how their heads turned slowly to follow after him or how they got that distant, dreamy look in their own eyes when he came close. Like a lot of good golfers, Sandy was just a big kid who found a game he didn't have to give up and who never really wanted to grow up at all. The two of us played miniature golf with our dinner once—peas for balls and carrot sticks for clubs; I nearly beat him too.

Now Sandy's blue eyes were flashing. He'd seen Beast lose his temper and he sensed that opportunity was at hand. With a giant, arcing swing of the driver just in front of Beast's nose, Sandy issued a challenge.

"Come on, Larsen. Let's see what you got." He swung the club again, harder this time. "How 'bout a little game of chicken?"

Beast cracked his knuckles loudly.

"You're on, weenie!"

I didn't even know what they were talking about.

Sandy stuck a tee into the ground between them and they both stepped into a wide-anchored version of their golf stances, facing each other about six feet apart. They waggled their clubheads and set them face-to-face on opposite sides of the tiny wooden tee, golfers and clubheads both staring at each other intently.

Finally I figured it out. It was like playing chicken with cars, where two idiots drive straight at each other and whoever turns off first is the chicken. Only the golf clubs would be moving a lot faster than speeding cars. This seemed like an exceedingly stupid thing to do. I ducked down behind Beast's bag and peeked around for a look. Everybody else, including Jewel, stepped *way* back.

They both took a little warm-up; feeble swings about like wedge shots. The clubheads passed by each other safely, but it still looked plenty scary to me.

"You ready?" asked Beast with a wicked grin.

"Let's do it," answered Sandy.

Just as they started to swing, Roscoe interrupted: "A hundred on the Beast."

"Covered," said March.

Fromholz took the money from each of them, and now that he'd been made the ref in this contest as well, he stepped forward to insure that everything was in order.

"Don't kill yourselves off," Fromholz told them before scampering safely away.

Working up their nerves again, both took their clubheads back. With no worries as to where a ball might go and their only concern whether or not to chicken out, they were free to swing as hard as they wanted or were able. That's exactly what they did: two huge, powerful, simultaneous swats.

Neither chickened out. Instead both screamed mightily as the clubheads met head-to-head in an incredible explosion of wood and steel. Splinters of persimmon and hot metal shards flew in all directions. Sandy bent over with a groan while Beast merely grimaced, his hands vibrating like church bells.

"Well, I'd have to rule that a draw," said Fromholz. "How about two out of three?"

Neither of them seemed so inclined (or had another driver), so Roscoe snatched his money back.

"Don't worry about it, partner," he said to Beast. "Some days you eat the chicken; some days you eat the feathers."

Smelling something like burnt flesh, I looked down at Beast's bag and found two finger-size holes where flying hot metal from one of their shafts had torn through the leather.

Sandy still had ahold of his grip, with most of the shaft attached, but the head of his driver was no more; it had completely disintegrated. He spiked the shaft into the ground and shook off his pain the way basketball coaches told you to after you'd broken a couple of fingers or had your nose flattened. Then he took out his three-wood and hit a great shot up the fairway of the long par five.

"Oh! That's how you do it!" complimented March. Then he teed one up, swung easy, and hit his straight down the middle as well.

Beast stuck his big paw in my face. "Gimme my three-wood," he growled.

I hesitated, not sure I'd heard him right.

"Gimme my goddamn three-wood! Are you deaf?"

Taking out the two pieces of his three-wood that he'd smashed against the tree on number four, I held them out to him. He looked at the pieces like they were from Mars. I guess between the snake in the grass and the cup popping out of the ground, he'd forgotten all about breaking his fairway wood. A wave of understanding swept his face as he realized what Sandy's game of chicken had really been about.

"I'll beat you with a one-iron, smart-ass," Beast said to Sandy. But I got the feeling he didn't believe it.

I HAD A HARD time keeping my mind on the job at hand as we walked up the sixth fairway, climbing a long, slow hill like all the holes on the course. It's hard to figure how, but somebody built that course so you'd always be walking uphill. It felt like we'd end up about a mile higher than we started, but I didn't give a hoot 'cause I was just about tickled pink with the way things were turning out.

I believed then that a golf course was some sort of magic spot. The only places I'd ever been happy were sitting down at Jewel's dinner table or walking on the golf course. Seemed like everywhere else I went, either some kid was bragging about the neat stuff he'd been doing with his dad, or people were talking about something shitty that had happened. To me it sounded like there must be a lot of crummy goings on, and I had begun to suspect that the world was not as nice a place as everyone would have a kid believe.

From what they told me, Texas was supposed to be just about the greatest place on earth, but that hadn't kept Jewel from being lonely—sometimes I used to hear her crying softly in the night—and it hadn't even kept my mother Martha from going to some other place where she didn't have to think about me or any of her other troubles—and she always had plenty. Seemed to me

like no one ever had enough rain or money or good times, but
there was always plenty of trouble—trouble at school, trouble at
home, trouble with a bunch of nosy neighbors who were having
trouble with the bill collectors who were having trouble with
their wives and girlfriends who were all having trouble finding a
good hairdresser or a Mexican housekeeper to do their dirty
work for them.

I didn't understand why, if Texas was such a great place, all
the Mexicans had to live in such crummy houses in neighbor-
hoods that really were on the other side of the railroad tracks.
Everybody called it Mezkin town. There weren't any paved
streets or sewer lines, so when it rained the whole place just
turned into a mud hole, and if it rained enough it turned into a
shit hole. Then everybody on this side of the tracks would start
complaining about the gawd-awful smell coming from Mezkin
town and how can them people live like that?

About the only answer anybody ever had for that question was
that "those people wouldn't live any other way if they could."
That was just the way they were. Hell, if you put in a bunch of
paved driveways and fancy toilets, they'd still go right on parking
their cars in the grass and doing their business in the bushes or
the outhouse, at least that's what folks said. Besides, if you gave
'em an inch, they'd start wanting to live in the regular neighbor-
hoods and send their kids to the regular schools where they
wouldn't know how to speak no English and they'd just cause a
bunch of trouble anyway. And the last thing anybody needed was
any more damn trouble!

That was what I could never figure. If the world was such a
fine place to live—especially our corner of the world—then how
come everybody had so darn much trouble in mind?

Now all of a sudden I was looking at the other side of the
coin. Everything that had been tails was about to come up heads.

Beast was licked; you could tell it by the way he talked. Before when he bragged, it seemed as factual as if you had read it in the newspaper, and there was a chance that you would read it the next day.

Now it sounded sort of hollow. "I'll beat you with a one-iron," he said, but it sounded more like, "If I don't beat you, nobody can blame me. All I got is a one-iron."

The tide had definitely turned. Roscoe was about half looped on Jewel's whiskey, so there wasn't a doubt in my mind that March and Sandy were going to win the match. Sandy was going to take his winnings, go out on the Tour, and make a potful of money. He'd be famous and I'd probably be his caddie at the Masters and the Crosby out at Pebble Beach, and at the British Open at St. Andrews where March had learned to play.

March and Jewel were finally going to be man and wife, and since Jewel had been my mother, that meant March was going to be my father. I could call him Dad if I wanted, but I wouldn't 'cause March was the coolest name going.

Maybe we'd all move out to Sonora and drill some oil wells and open up that old golf course again. If Sandy was too rich and famous to be the head pro, then maybe Fromholz could take the job, or maybe someday I could. In the meantime March could take me horseback riding and camping, and on New Year's Eve and the Fourth of July, the three of us—my family and I—could drive down to Villa Acuña for a big celebration with fireworks and mariachis.

It was all going to be great fun, and I wasn't gonna have any more trouble in mind, that's what I decided. I was all through with trouble in mind.

Book Two

Walk tall and loose,

carrying your club at your side,

as you go toward your ball.

—COUNT YOGI

IN TRYING TO UNDERSTAND what happened then, I've gone "own and own" (as March would've said) about who I used to be, but I haven't even hinted at who I am now, these twenty-five years later. Perhaps the point is, who I am now is the product of what happened to me then. Suffice it to say that I've never been able to get any of it out of my head or my heart, and I guess the truth is, I never really wanted to.

I dreamed of March last night; of what he told me and what I learned in the too-short time that I knew him. In my dream March was young, like in the photo with the horses that he'd taken down off the wall of his office and presented to me as a gift that day it all began. Even in the dream I remembered that March's horse was the Appaloosa. Jewel was with him, and her age was undefined—timeless—just the way I always think of her; her cheeks like roses and her hair like fine silk. March kept trying to tell me something; it was terribly important but I couldn't understand what he was saying, and Jewel brushed my hair back out of my eyes and repeated over and over, "That's right. That's exactly right. You'll find out sooner or later that he's right." But I never did understand what they were trying to tell me.

It was raining when I awoke; the middle of the night. I heard the water dripping from the roof, dripping, it seemed, in sweat upon my brow, then running a salty trickle down my nose like a tear. I knew it would be quite a while before I could sleep again.

I thought about March and Jewel and the love they shared; undying in both their hearts through thirty years of separation and in my own mind for another twenty-five years after, and I wondered how it is that man survives the misery of circumstance and the burden of regret. March would have said that it was like surviving the scarcity of rain: by hoarding more, by needing less.

A distant flash of lightning illuminated the room for a moment, and I considered getting up to check on my son, five years old and just learning a fear of thunder. But it wasn't loud enough to wake him, so I decided against turning on the light and bothering my wife, a sound and happy sleeper. Insomnia is not an affliction to be shared.

As the rain grew heavier I wondered how I'd ever be able to tell my boy what March had meant to me. I figure I owe that much to both of them. I've already told Squirt parts of it; shown him the photo and explained about playing golf and riding horses, but none of it seems real to him—they're just bedtime stories. Sometimes, though, he'll be about to doze off and some detail will fascinate his idling mind and pull him back from Sandland.

"Poppy! You were an Indian?"

"No, Squirt. I just looked like one. Now hush up. If you get some sleep you can go out to the course with me in the morning."

"Can I take my golf club?"

"You bet you can."

The game goes on: his one treasured club, a cut-down ladies' five-iron. He whales away at the ball, and though it doesn't go far, like the shot of a very old golfer, it often sails straight and true, demanding that you marvel at the miraculous flight.

The thunder began to move away and with it the chance of a real soaking rain. In Texas the best part of the storm is always somewhere else. I lay quietly in the dark and in my mind I played a near-perfect nine holes of golf, nine holes at the Pedernales Golf Club just the way it was, and just the way it is now, essentially unchanged this quarter-century later, though perhaps the greens are no longer as fast. Each shot was crystal clear in my mind. My drives split the fairways and my crisp irons bit nicely at each and every pin. The making of the putts, if I paid the proper attention to a light grip and a square clubface, were mere formalities.

Nine under through eight holes, with only the long par four remaining, I began to wonder what the course record was for an imaginary round. And though the south breeze at the end of the storm blew fresh in my face, the fluid swings were rapidly sending me from insomnia to dreamland. I stood over the ball, driver in hand, and lazily dragged the clubhead back. My legs were already asleep, so I blocked the shot, cutting a huge bending slice right out of my childhood, my drive soaring from the fairway into the driving range. With my ball lost among thousands of range balls, I waded through them searching for that single one without a stripe, desperate to finish a perfect round of golf that only my mind kept from completion. But before I found the ball, I was fast asleep.

"Even a blind hog finds an acorn once in a while."

That's what Roscoe said when he hit his ball up close to the sixth green from what he called "the seven-iron pole." Actually the big telephone pole he was talking about was way over on the far edge of the rough, but Roscoe had been lying about even with it.

"It's the only place on the whole danged course I know what club to use."

If he'd been twenty-five yards inside the seven-iron pole, he'd probably have chipped backwards so he could hit that seven-iron with some confidence. Golf does strange things to the brain.

Now Roscoe was hitting a little chip shot, and from the look of things, he really was rooting around for acorns, 'cause he looked up, chili-dipped, burped and farted all at a time.

"Same damn dummy hit that shot as the last one," he said, again taking a long pull on the bottle of whiskey Jewel had brought him.

"And all your other shitty ones too," added Beast.

Sandy was next. He'd flown in a long, high four-wood that just caught the top edge of a trap at the front of the green. The ball was buried so completely in the sand that we'd first thought it lost.

"You might be able to chip it out sideways," suggested March when he discovered the ball, which showed itself only as a nickel-size circle of white peeking out from the sand.

"No time to play it safe," answered Sandy.

Wedge in hand, his right foot down in the trap and left foot up on the lip, Sandy cocked the clubhead and lifted it straight up to ear level. Then, without uncocking his wrists, he moved the club, his arms and his shoulders as one powerful unit into the ball. As the clubhead came up, it was accompanied by a giant gouge, not just of sand, but of the entire lip of the trap: grass, dirt, beach and all. The ball lofted to about ten feet from the pin and stuck like a lawn dart. After a beat, the giant divot landed next to the ball.

"Aye, laddie!" asked Fromholz. "Be ye digging for pirate treasure?"

"You bet he is," said March.

Beast's birdie attempt was from fifteen feet. He must've been losing confidence because he threw his cigarette away before he putted. Then he licked his lips and lipped the putt out as well.

"Son," says Roscoe, "you been gettin' lots of nibbles but not many fish!"

I don't think March even lined his up. A lot of golfers swear by the plumb-bob method: holding the putter loosely below the grip with thumb and middle finger, then extending the arm so that the lower part of the dangling putter is in line with the ball and the hole. All you have to do then is close one eye, look through the other, and see whether the upper part of the putter shaft indicates to the right or left of the hole. Take into consideration the grain of the grass, the lawnmower cut, and maybe even the wind, and then you know *exactly* where to putt the ball— about a third of the time. March had his own method: aim right at the hole and hope for the best.

This putt must've been a straight one because it looked perfect all the way to the hole and even more so after it dropped. Perhaps not trusting his own eyes, March glanced around in surprise. When it dawned on him that he'd actually made a birdie, he tossed his putter aside, knelt down, and did a little frogstyle headstand on the green, singing another of his twisted songs.

"Grab your goat and get your cat. Get the puppies off your doorstep—"

"With three holes to go," interrupted Fromholz.

"Let them do their deeds—"

"The match is even."

Before March could finish his song, he lost his balance and fell over on his ass.

"You okay?" asked Sandy, leaning over him.

March opened his eyes and picked up the beat: *"On the other side of the street."*

I thought his act was even better than Ronny and Donny, the Siamese twins I'd seen at the rodeo sideshow in San Angelo. "They were born to die, but God let them live!" trumpeted the banner. It cost me fifty cents to get in and all they did was eat donuts, watch *Gunsmoke* on TV, and make fun of my big ears. Truly I didn't mind being awkwardly skinny and tall, but I loathed my gigantic ears and dreaded being called Dumbo, which was, of course, the name that either Ronny or Donny hit upon for me.

Beast could have hit me two-for-flinching when he stomped up to me with his putter, but for once he was mad at someone else. Easing the putter into the bag, he strolled over to Roscoe's cart and violently wrenched the almost empty whiskey bottle out of his partner's hand.

"Are you nuts?" screamed Beast. "Twenty grand on the line and you're blotto!"

I figured Roscoe was fixing to go for the little pistol I'd seen peeking out of his bag, but being a drilling boss, he must've handled guys like Beast before.

"How dare you yell at me, you fat ape!" he hollered in the big man's face. "You're my trained monkey, remember? My dumb-ass jerk of a hit man. And why is that? Because I put up the cash! So when I want to have a drink, I have a drink. And when I say 'Hit it at the pin,' you hit it at the pin! Otherwise keep your ugly mouth shut!"

Beast stared coldly at his partner. There weren't many possible responses to a lecture like that. It looked to me as if Beast was deciding between keeping his mouth shut or killing Roscoe right then and there.

But before Beast could do anything, Roscoe turned his back as if to say "dismissed," then sat heavily in his cart.

"Come on, Jewel, hop in."

Jewel looked somewhat disinterested.

"You go ahead," she told him.

"Then hop in with me," said March. "I got a spot on my dance card."

"Gentlemen," she said. "Just now, nobody seems to be winning. I think I'll walk a spell."

Then she latched her hand onto the crook of Fromholz's arm and the two of them strolled on beneath the shade of her parasol, while Roscoe and March fumed in the hot Texas sun.

28

NOW THAT MARCH AND Sandy were bound to win (I could *smell* it), they no longer even needed my help. Shouldering Beast's bag, I dropped two dutiful paces behind him, glad that I could quit worrying and just enjoy the day. The seventh tee had been built atop the highest hill on the course, and the view that was afforded us there was thirty miles in all directions.

On two quarters, east and south, was the winding body of Lake Travis, named for Colonel William B. Travis, defender of the Alamo. You remember the Alamo, don't you? Well, it is Lake Travis's job to make sure we remember the colonel. And that day he was pretty unforgettable. Several miles across and too far away to reveal the shimmering of the waves or the wakes of the few sailors and bass fisherman, the lake instead showed us a deep indigo blue, motionless, as if it had been painted there.

To the north and west were the river basins themselves, the Colorado (the *Texas* Colorado) and its tributary, the Pedernales: immense valleys spotted to their horizons in the various greens of oaks, cedar, and grasses that would within a month be burned to a crisp by the summer sun.

From our distant vantage you'd never have known that the entire vista was populated not just by the normal array of ranch animals—cattle, sheep and goats—but also by millions of wild animals: white-tailed deer, wild turkeys, javelinas (a south Texas peccary with big teeth and a nasty disposition), beavers, bobcats, badgers, porcupines, possums, raccoons, and prehistoric armadillos. The four hundred species of birds varied from majestic bald eagles and great blue herons to the tiny black-capped vireos and colorful painted buntings. And of all these animals, only a small minority would ever be seen by a human.

Yet we call that land our land. We issue covenants that bestow and convey the right to occupy and utilize it according to our need, to subjugate and cultivate according to our want, and to obliterate or ameliorate according to our whim. Then we convey that right according to our lineage, our greed, or to the roll of the dice or the drop of a curling putt.

A man dreams of owning such land because the use or abuse of it is one of the truest tests of his character and disposition. That, coupled with how he treats his family, friends, partners and enemies, in the same manner that the ball indicates the measure of the golf swing, indicates the measure of the man.

March, having missed nearly a lifetime with what should have been his family and his land (far across those hills to the northwest), had apparently one day taken his measure and come up sorely lacking. Although somewhat late, he was now on the verge of changing all that, reclaiming what was his no matter what the cost. Deep inside me I could feel my breath swelling up and lifting my heart to him. Somehow I just couldn't help but love him.

Roscoe obviously didn't share my emotion. As March drove his cart leisurely toward the seventh tee, Roscoe pulled his own buggy up tightly against March's back bumper and stepped on the gas. Hoping to outrun him, March also stepped on the gas, but Roscoe's cart was faster and both carts raced forward in tandem.

"I'm on your butt, cowboy," Roscoe screamed like a madman. "Now git outta my way!"

We all jumped back as the two carts sped by, hooked together like two dragonflies in passionate copulation. Rounding a curve in the path, first March's cart, then Roscoe's, leaned out on two wheels. Just as I thought they were goners, both carts straightened up and slammed back down on all fours.

"Yeee-high!!!" screamed Roscoe.

Coming to the elevated tee, Roscoe stomped on the brakes of his cart and screeched sideways to a halt. March's cart rocketed forward over the ridge and launched into the air.

We were running toward him when the cart bounced twice and March wrestled it to a halt at the edge of a precipitous dropoff. He looked over the edge at his near fate, then drove the near-crippled cart back up the hill to the tee where Roscoe was roaring with laughter.

"Whoooeee! March, you flew further than your average drive!" laughed Roscoe. "I was watching you like you wuz a hawk!"

March laughed along with Roscoe for a moment, then both slowed their laughter till nothing was left but their heavy breathing and a mutual stare. Roscoe wasn't sure what March was going to do.

March smiled broadly. Relieved, Roscoe smiled too.

Then without warning, March coldcocked Roscoe with a gigantic sucker punch to the nose. Roscoe went down as if a pickpocket had lifted his spinal cord. March just stood there over him, breathing hard, exhausted, unnerved, and wrenched by tiny spasms as his hand reached slowly to his chest.

"I owed you that, Roscoe," he said through the pain. "I owed you that for thirty years."

*   *   *

I never knew exactly what March owed Roscoe for thirty years. Was he literally talking about a punch in the nose? Or was he figuratively talking about the fact that Roscoe had so brazenly screwed March out of their company and his own land. Neither of them denied that March had shot Roscoe in the leg, near crippling him for life, and you'd think that an additional punch in the nose after all that time would have had little effect on the score they seemed to be keeping.

But when Roscoe came groggily to his senses on that lofty seventh tee, the two of them began a deadly downhill momentum that would finally bring them head-to-head over the bitterness they'd harbored through the years. Empty insults and verbal back-stabbing would no longer suffice. Nor would settling their case through a couple of golfing surrogates like Beast and Sandy. This time it was for real. And even though I didn't understand all of what transpired—not just then anyway—it wouldn't take long for me to get a grasp on the big picture, to finally realize why Jewel cried out for them to just *stop*! Stop the fighting, the arguing, the animosity. And stop the eternal quest for revenge and one-upmanship that had come to define a once-great friendship that had simply turned to shit.

The problem was—those thirty years ago in West Texas—that Jewel fancied herself such an independent young woman, that March was downright stubborn, and of course that Roscoe was such a prick.

The problem was that Jewel didn't want to have the baby she was carrying, despite the fact that March professed to be tickled pink about the situation. So Jewel lied; telling March that to avoid any chance of gossip getting back to her father, they should cross the border and visit a Mexican doctor for a check on the health of their unborn. March must have been naive to drive her to Mexico and wait patiently in the dirty reception room while Jewel's so-called examination began. I can imagine him there, blissful in ignorance, musing on being a father—things he'd do with his child; things to teach; things to learn.

And I can also see his eyes opening wide for a real look at the squalid clinic, the realization of what the place was and what they were doing there. A locked door wouldn't stop March, not to save his child, and perhaps to save Jewel as well. Apparently he barged in with only moments to spare, and over Jewel's protests, March carried her and the tiny life inside her to safety.

But a flimsy door was less of an obstacle than Jewel's determination which remained unswayed. Was it that she felt too young to have a baby? Did she fear the wrathful judgment and accusing finger of her father? Or did she just not want to be tied down?

No, the problem was that Jewel wasn't sure whose baby it was. Perhaps she told that to March as he carried her from the clinic; I don't really know. It would have been like him to say he didn't care—but it would have also been like him to have cared very much.

Not a single word passed between the two during the three-hour drive back to Sonora. And during that long and oppressive silence, both knew that something between them had changed. So when March and Jewel arrived back at the well, with the procedure aborted instead of the baby, Jewel did the only thing her white hot rage at March would allow: she asked Roscoe if he was sick of that smelly dry hole they'd been pumping. When he said "Hell, yes!" the two of them—Jewel and Roscoe—climbed into the same dusty pickup in which the trouble had all begun and drove away. I don't know if Roscoe punched March before they left; maybe that was what March owed him. All I know is, Roscoe took Jewel away, and March didn't see her again for thirty years.

That was the problem.

WHETHER ROSCOE DESERVED IT or not, March had given him one heck of a bloody nose, and it just wouldn't stop running red. He sat there between the blue markers of the seventh tee, soaking his handkerchief in blood, and sputtering how he hadn't asked for any of this. The only thing he did wrong, he mumbled, was to cheat at the cut of the cards so he could go to the Wing Ding instead of March.

This didn't even get a raised eyebrow from March, who had sagged down next to Roscoe. They looked like a pitiful pair of aging boxers, too weak to punch or even to get back to their corners. The one thing they had in common was that they both looked worn-out to the point of extinction.

When I met them, they'd only looked a little over the hill, and that was in relation to my tender years. Now, in addition to being bloody, Roscoe's face was yellow and puffy, not just from the punch, but from the emotion, the whiskey, and perhaps from the faint idea sloshing around in his pickled brain that he'd lived long enough in that damned Texas sun.

March, besides being pale and clammy, looked sort of shrunken and withered. I'd fetched the little bottle of pills from his golf bag, quickly given him two, then returned the medicine to its proper place. But March was not reviving the way he had earlier. The both of them looked like death's rejections, leftovers from the pickings of the devil that only a buzzard would touch.

I turned to Jewel to see if she'd noticed as well, and for the first time I had ever seen, she wasn't all beautiful and shining. She just looked very, very sad. And instead of stepping closer to be a part of things, she stepped back where she wouldn't be noticed, I suppose to hide the tears that were slowly rolling down her cheeks.

"It's a good thing we're only playing nine," March gasped.

"Nine holes is for babies," said Beast, trying to reignite the game and his possible fortune. "We oughta be playing eighteen."

"Son!" said Fromholz. "The gods made the game eighteen holes because the first nine you play against the course and the second nine you play against yourself."

"So?"

"So you don't have to play eighteen 'cause you've already played against yourself."

"Up yours!" said Beast. "Let's play some golf."

Roscoe finally stopped his nosebleed by stuffing a plug of chewing tobacco into his damaged nostril, and March climbed up off the ground with only a little assist from me. Neither of them, however, was in any shape to swing a club. Sensing that he'd lost control of the match, Fromholz ruled that the pros would play the hole alone. Then Beast and Sandy both hit good shots down to the bottom of the big hill.

Trying to referee for March and Roscoe was like orchestrating an insane asylum. Just the technical details were beginning to test Fromholz's patience. March's cart was now sitting seriously askew—the landing from the trip aloft having bent the axle beyond repair—so Fromholz shifted March's clubs to Roscoe's cart. Roscoe refused to ride with March, who was in no condition to walk, so Jewel was enlisted to be March's driver.

"Hold up!" Roscoe hollered to Jewel as she passed by us in the fairway. "Forgot my chew."

Roscoe limped over to the cart and I handed Beast his eight-iron. Then I remembered that Roscoe had used his tobacco on the tee and hadn't returned to the cart since. I turned around, and for a brief moment I could've sworn that he was digging around in March's bag instead of his own. I would have said something—oh, how I wished I had—but when I looked at March to see if he'd noticed, I lost the thought. For March's mind had wandered to greener pastures and fairer shores, one final aimless journey of heart and soul, marked only by a faint mumbling delirium.

Drawing closer, as if in a dream myself, I gazed into his sad blue eyes, and I became his witness, an involuntary eavesdropper on the final tally of his life, the way it had been, and the way it might have been as well; March shivering in a stream of icy water, at last a well spewing artesian life instead of smelly oil. It must have tasted sweet as he pursed his lips, tasted sweet like a long putt topping a rise, gathering speed, and rushing toward the heart of the hole. He was humming to the *norteño* music playing in the background, and Jewel must have been radiant in her white-lace Mexican wedding dress. Lovingly, Jewel had once taken the dress from her closet and shown it to me, telling me its story. The sleepy *señorita* who owned the shop had held a lantern as Jewel twirled and spun, her hair and the hem of the dress all whirling with dancing, dervish shadows that reflected in March's eyes. And then he was looking out again from the Scottish Lowlands to the brooding sea. And the bagpipes resounded from off the stone (or perhaps from within it), and he recalled the nun's funny little accordion as it sang "Here Comes the Bride" in a minor key while the unshaven Mexican priest beseeched the Lord on high in Latin and in Spanish. March's murmuring was racing in a stream of unconsciousness that had his sad-eyed alcoholic father looking down from the back of the chapel upon his son about to be wed, and for the last time March would ever envision, his father smiled. Smiled so that March could feel the tears streaming down his face as Jewel gripped his hand tightly and said, "¡Sí! I do take this man. I do." And in his reverie they were lying together in the coming dawn, lovers, wrapped in a huge pile of Mexican *serapes* and colorful handwoven blankets, lying soft upon skin that moves softly on skin softer still. And somewhere his numbed brain or tired soul began to glow, the light approaching from the east to the top of this sacred hill. The darkness fled from their touch, Jewel sighed with the wind, and March knew for the first time since his father died that the God in heaven can also be found on earth. . . .

And suddenly Jewel's voice is saying, "William, oh please, William, are you all right?"

His eyes, still without focus, flickered with a little smile, then his lips moved like the wind on a calm day, and the highest leaves of the tallest trees rustled a faint "I love you."

Jewel put her arms around his neck, hugging for all the lost hugs, then spoke softly back to him, her words seeking out the place where he'd gone to hide.

"William March. You come back here this minute; there's people here that love you." Then after a pause to sniffle back a tear, she added, "I love you."

He was more than one foot down in that grave; both legs were in and sinking fast, but he summoned a wildcatter's strength long forgotten and pulled himself up out of the dead earth just as surely as he had so many times sucked up long-dead dinosaurs or eons of whale urine or whatever it was he'd spent his life pumping up from out of the old rock. When his eyes began to focus, he breathed deeply, smelled the hot dust on the living wind, and almost smiled.

He still didn't know where he was, not at first. He looked at us like the strangers we mostly were, and slowly it came to him that he was seated there in the cart next to Jewel on the seventh fairway of a long road home. And for each of his tears, there were tears on Jewel's cheeks to match.

Sandy stepped up close. "March, you okay?"

"Sure," he said. "I'm fine." He turned to Jewel. "It's just that I been a long time alone. A long time. But it won't be long now."

THINGS DID NOT IMPROVE after Jewel and Roscoe abandoned March that day at the well, because none of them had actually gotten what they wanted, a sad state of affairs they all seemed unable to admit.

For starters, Roscoe's lotharial conquest had been just that, a victory, much as losing Jewel to March had simply been a loss. Spending the first fifteen years of his life in a Galveston orphanage had given Roscoe a sense of the score. Those who slept in top bunks and ate at the head of the line were winners. Those who slept on the bottom and scraped the pail were little more than bed wetters and beggars. Life was not meant to be spent on the bottom bunk.

A semifamous wildcatter like Roscoe drew occasional attention from the Texas press; after all, he was successful local color. One of the newspaper interviews—in Roscoe's own words— told how at age fifteen he'd broken into the office of the orphanage that dared to call itself his home. Discovering whose monthly checks were paying his bill, he escaped his toy prison and hitchhiked to Houston. There he confronted H. R. Hughes: inventor, oilman, and founder of the Hughes Tool Company (which made millions manufacturing the rolling cone drill bit, invented by H.R. himself).

Being smart and tough himself, it wasn't hard for Roscoe to conclude that he was indeed sprung without consent from the loins of the famous manufacturer, but there was a complication. H.R. already had a son, Howard Hughes, Jr., future aviation pioneer, moviemaker, and proverbial chip off the old block. Not knowing that Howard junior would eventually become an emaciated, germ-fearing billionaire-recluse, H.R. was somewhat less than ecstatic at Roscoe's arrival.

Denying knowledge of any young bastards, H.R. offered the teenager two choices. Have the crap beat out of him before being tossed out on his ear. Or have the crap beat out of him, then work as an apprentice welder and tool dresser. H.R. had in mind an unproved test well in Big Lake, Texas, which was about as far from Houston as you could get and not be under the legal jurisdiction of another state where Hughes didn't own the law.

If keeping score wasn't already the dominant influence in Roscoe's life, it didn't take long as bottom boy on Santa Rita Number One to tattoo it into his soul. The experience must have hardened him like steel. Even for a seasoned roughneck, the work was long, tough, dirty and dangerous. For a boy, it must have been almost inhuman.

Santa Rita Number One eventually spewed a million gallons of the creamiest crude the world had ever tasted.

"Its specific gravity was so high," Roscoe boasted decades later, "that a refinery was redundant. One day the foreman's truck ran out of gas, so I put in a couple gallons of crude right off the wellhead, and it *ran*, better than before!"

He could burn it in the boss's truck, but that was the closest he'd ever come to owning it. Not that Roscoe or his bone-tired fellow workers wanted to change the natural order. No, they weren't interested in none of that commie labor organizing. Oh no, the way to make things better was to tell the boss to shove twenty feet of casing in an alternate location where the sun don't shine, then get the hell out and drill your own damn well!

That's what took Roscoe, then in his twenties, to the hills above the Dry Devil's River, where William March swore there was oil beneath his very own land, known since March's dad's lonely and booze-laden final years as the Devil's Sanctuary.

It was there that Roscoe and March founded a business based on that famous Texas sentiment that a man's word is as good as his bond. Their deal was sealed by a handshake, less between geologist-owner and drilling contractor than between two men who were bound to act as honestly as they expected to be treated. Of course, that was before they made the acquaintance of Miss Jewel Anne Hemphill. That was before March really knew Roscoe at all.

Once Jewel abandoned March in favor of Roscoe, the score became two to one in Roscoe's favor. As far as he was concerned, the contest was over. After a few weeks, Roscoe got bored with his amour. And when he found out she was pregnant, he walked out on her. Where did Roscoe go? Where else? Back to the oil business. Back to March.

But things change. In Roscoe's absence, March had somehow managed to keep the crew working without pay. He worked double and triple shifts himself to cover for those who did leave, and he kept the whole operation going twenty-four hours a day. Every minute of it, they were firing that old boiler with mesquite and cedar stumps so they could keep sinking the bit, adding a pipe, and sinking the bit, ad infinitum. The only break in the routine was when the time came to pull the bit and remove a pipe—over and over for the whole damn drilling string—so that they could sink more casing to chase their progress downward. There was no due date, no known gestation period for this baby, indeed no guarantee that the damn well would come in at all.

Nothing really to know for sure except that Jewel was gone and that the hole wanted deepening, was practically crying out for another length of pipe. All the while, March schemed to float the food, tobacco and whiskey bills, and kept drilling so that he didn't have to think about anything but landing that bit in gumbo, which, with a lot of cursing and coaxing, he finally did.

The well didn't come in a showy gusher the way March had hoped, but it was a steady flow; a moneymaker sitting in a potential field of moneymakers. And as far as March was concerned, not a penny or a drop of it belonged to that back-stabbing bastard Roscoe.

Some folks call it a timeless land; some think of it as behind the times. In any event, the Indians hadn't been murdered or run out of West Texas until the late nineteenth century, and most of the folks of the region hardly noticed the twentieth century arrive. In the Sutton County of the early thirties a horse was often more reliable transportation than a car, and a gun was just another of the tools, like a hammer or an ax, that you grew up learning to use. So when Roscoe returned to demand his share of the well, there was only one way to settle their differences: the old-fashioned way.

March selected a lever-action .30-30, not real fast but deadly accurate, and Roscoe foolishly ignored the shotgun in favor of the traditional Colt six-shooter.

It was an affair of honor. The referee was Uncle Piggy, the alcoholic nitro man who had days earlier blasted the well into production with a nitro torpedo—loading a metal canister with twenty gallons of liquid nitro, dropping it into the well, and running like hell. Ten seconds of free-fall silence was followed by a deep, rumbling explosion that fragmented the subterranean rock in all directions and allowed the nearby oil to come to the surface under the pressure of the field.

Like all nitro men, Uncle Piggy's problem was his persistent headaches—brain damage really—brought on by breathing glycerin, and temporarily relieved only by massive and steady doses of alcohol. Between the melted brain cells, decaying liver, and your occasional accidental explosion, the career expectancy for a nitro man was about four years. Uncle Piggy had been at it for fourteen.

He did his damndest to load the wrong bullets into the right guns, and then tried to reverse it and load the right bullets into the wrong guns. At last Roscoe and March each loaded their own—one bullet each—then the pair declined to shake hands and impatiently walked several paces apart.

Uncle Piggy tried to count to ten but kept having to start over at four. Roscoe fired first and missed. With the leisure of time on his side, March drew a steady bead on Roscoe's hard heart, but at the last minute, he just didn't have it in him. As he pulled the trigger, March jerked the gun down toward the ground. Though he was attempting to miss, he still blew off Roscoe's kneecap.

It was months before Roscoe was able to walk again (and even then with a hobble he'd never shake). In the meantime, March's guilt took over. Maybe it really wasn't Roscoe's fault. After all, from the first night at the Wing Ding, Miss Jewel Anne Hemphill had been the foundation of a house divided. By virtue of countenance and deed, by way of innocence and vanity, she had driven a festering wedge between the two friends.

God, what had he done? March had almost killed his pal; he'd crippled him for life over some kind of horrible jealous love or infatuation. It was like a sickness both of them had contracted, an infection of the heart, a poisoning. That was it: they'd been snakebit.

There was no righting the kind of wrong that March had done to Roscoe, but he did the best he could and gave back half the well, indeed half of that well and all future wells. They'd be partners again. And they'd be friends. At least they'd try.

As for Jewel—well, March only wanted her if she needed him, or cared for him. She was bound to write, he thought, but he received no word.

THE SHADOW OF A small, billowy cloud, the mid-morning edition of what would later be a rumbling thunderstorm, floated toward us and momentarily cast its cool relief across the seventh fairway. The shade wasn't much, but it was enough to bring March back to life. Or perhaps he'd simply come to a decision that would finally bring things to a conclusion one way or the other. Pulling an iron from his bag, he tossed a ball down in the fairway.

"What the hell are you doing?" asked Roscoe.

"I thought I'd get back in the hole," March answered.

"Well, it's too late for that, honcho! You tell him, Fromholz. No scramblin'! No mulligans! No damn cheatin'!"

March hadn't even hit a tee shot, so for once Fromholz had to agree with Roscoe.

"What's up, March?" Fromholz asked.

March told Fromholz to bring out the thirty-year-old scorecard from the first match and Fromholz produced it.

"Notice anything funny about it?" March asked.

"Yes sir! I been meaning to ask you about that. Roscoe won with an ace on the last hole? That would have to be the most miraculous shot in the history of golf!"

"Oh, it was more than a miracle," March assured us.

"What the hell's that supposed to mean?" Roscoe demanded to know as he limped toward March with just a little more hobble than usual. "You saying I cheated? After all these years, you're saying I cheated?"

"Hold it! Just wait a dang minute," said Beast. "How does a guy cheat to make a hole-in-one? Either it goes in or it don't go in. What, were you guys blind?"

"Well, big man," said March, "as a matter of fact we were blind, 'cause it can get real dark when you're playing at night."

"At night!" Beast threw up his hands in surrender. "You're both looney-tunes!"

"I don't get it either," added Sandy. "Why would you play a big match at night?"

"That's when we thought of it," said March.

"And it was too damn hot to play in the day," added Roscoe.

Just then the cloud moved on and the sun reappeared.

"Just like it's getting to be now. It'd been a hundred and ten every day for weeks. The glare was bright enough to sunburn your eyeballs."

"Besides," added March, "that way, Roscoe could cheat."

"You want me to admit it? Is that it? Okay! Fine!" trumpeted Roscoe. "I did cheat! I fixed your pants good, didn't I, March? And there's nothing you can do about it now, you dumb hillbilly. I found that ball in a patch of prickly pear and just dropped that sucker in the hole!"

March must have been waiting a long time for this confession, not just wanting to get even, but hoping to finally satisfy the doubts in his mind.

He shook his head sadly. "Christ, Roscoe, of course you cheated! We've played golf together once a week for twenty-seven years and you've cheated every damn time. If you weren't teeing it up in the rough you were finding out-of-bounds shots in the fairway. If you weren't neglecting to count a topped shot or a scooped chip, you were on the green marking your ball over and over, each time moving it a foot closer to the hole. It's the only way you've been able to stay in the game."

"Screw you!" said Roscoe.

"And you had to live with it, you sorry bastard! Just like you're the one that has to live with having run our company into the ground. It wasn't my field reports that bankrupted us. It was you trying to screw everybody in the oil business a second time after you already bent 'em over and poked 'em once before. And now we're just oil bidness history. It'd bother me if I knew I screwed the pooch, but since I was just along for the ride in your own little donkey show, I really don't shiv a git."

For the first time I'd ever seen, Roscoe was speechless.

When March had finished his little rant, he took a swing at the ball he'd dropped and caught it with a giant yanking hook that sent it farther left than ahead.

"Would you look at that! I'm a pitiful excuse for a sad sonuva-bitch myself. Like taking candy from a rube! I talk myself into a free shot and I blow it."

The rest of us just looked on helplessly while March laughed at his own sad self, then coughed and choked and laughed some more.

It was Jewel who calmed him, who took his hand and held it to her own soft face, who soothed him with gentle words as if he were a sick child or an injured dog. And it was Jewel who had a solution.

"March, it's not worth dying over," she told him. "Just drop it. Walk away. Come with me and start all over. Even if we can't be young, we can still manage carefree. But please, God, don't just stand there wasting away a little bit at a time. That's not what you want, is it?"

"No," said March, hanging his head.

"Well, it isn't what I want either. I'm tired of you two fighting over me anyway. In case you two old coots haven't noticed, I still have a certain amount of choice in the matter and my choice will always be you, March. So if I'm all you're fighting about, it's settled. Let's get out of here. Let's get out of here right now and start our lives over."

March took her hand away from his face and kissed it.

"That's good enough for me," he said.

For a moment the two of them might have been a little porcelain portrait of ageless love, then March led Jewel back to the cart and gallantly brushed the dirt off her seat.

"Sorry, Sandy. You're on you're own! But you don't need me to whip these mugs, anyway."

"Jewel!" ordered Roscoe, pushing her lightly to one side. "You stay out of this! It was never about you; it was always about him and me."

He pointed a stubby finger from March to himself.

"The better man, the tougher, the smarter, the meaner; and by God, it's just about over and I aim to see it through. March, after all these years, don't you even want to know who won?"

"You poor bastard," March said softly. "That may be what you thought it was about, but as far as I'm concerned, it was about Jewel. I never did get her out of my heart or my head. Every day and every night, I missed her. I miss her right now 'cause you're standing between us like always, you and your sense of being wronged. Drop it, man. Leave it alone. It's over. Finished. Done. Go drill your damn well in the North Sea or marry that woman Rowena who's always following after you, but get it through your head that whatever you do, it ain't gonna have nothing to do with us."

March tipped his hat to the rest of the group.

"Gentlemen, it's been interesting!"

"Hold it, hoss," said Roscoe. "I got something for you."

Roscoe moved to his bag at the back of the cart, opened a zipper, and stuck in his hand. I knew that little gun was in there and suddenly I realized that the only way out of this humiliation, the only way for Roscoe to preserve his twisted sense of honor, was to kill March.

"No!" I yelled.

All heads turned slowly and looked at me in surprise. Then Roscoe, muttering in disbelief at the general level of insanity, instead of a gun pulled out a wrinkled, faded envelope and waved it at March.

"I promised to deliver this to you," he said. "And if you leave now I might not see you again. I wouldn't want to go back on my word, ol' buddy!"

Jewel looked at the envelope like she'd been struck by lightning.

"Roscoe, you son of a bitch! You dirty rotten bastard! Thirty years! You ran off and left me, a homeless pregnant woman in the middle of the Depression, and all I asked was that you deliver this letter to March. You swore! You *swore* you'd do it."

"That's right," Roscoe admitted. "But I didn't say when."

Jewel took the letter from Roscoe and held it bunched in her hand.

"Oh, William!" she sobbed. "I'm so sorry! I kept waiting for you to come. I was just a girl and I didn't understand why you wouldn't come for me. Finally I decided you didn't want me. I would have come to you sooner or later, but not if you didn't want me."

March just looked at the letter blankly, like the rest of us, trying to understand what had happened.

"When Roscoe found out I was pregnant, he started packing and I wrote this letter for him to take to you."

Jewel tugged on the flap of the envelope. The decayed or broken seal flopped open and the letter tumbled out onto the seat of the cart. March picked it up and began to read.

" 'My dearest March, how can you ever forgive me? How could I not want to keep your child, our child—' "

"That's not what you told me it said!" Roscoe yelled. "You swore just like I did, but you lied too! And you kept writing those lies to March, didn't you? For months you wrote, but ol' Roscoe always picked up the mail. It was the only job fit for a cripple! You both thought I was some kind of fool you could just treat any way you wanted, but I showed you different, didn't I? Didn't I show you different?"

Jewel sobbed softly and March just stared at Roscoe for a long, long time.

"I can't leave yet, Jewel," March finally said, "not till I see this heartless bastard beat to the bone, and hear him say he's sorry."

MAYBE ALL THREE OF their lives would have taken better turns if Jewel had been certain who the father was; perhaps she'd have wanted that baby all along. But after Roscoe left her alone, some change came over Jewel. March became more important than her situation, and her baby became more important than anything.

There was one large Catholic convent in San Angelo, populated mostly by Latinas who had exchanged the harshness and poverty of the outside world for the harshness and boredom of a poor convent. When she walked up the dirt path to the heavy wooden gates, Jewel told me, she didn't know that the nuns hadn't taken in pregnant girls since times got so hard in 1930. Hers was a hope devoid of foundation, a plan lacking in fact. But while Jewel waited there to see the Mother Superior, she was visited by the one miracle of the entire affair. Not much showing her pregnancy and being better dressed than most supplicants of the day, she was mistaken as an applicant for the low-paying job of English teacher for the Spanish-speaking nuns, a job the Mother Superior had advertised in the *San Angelo Standard-Times* that very morning.

It was a good day for miracles. The front page of the paper was emblazoned for the first time in months with a page-high imprint of a large rooster, so big and red you could almost hear it crow. This same rooster has always appeared in the San Angelo paper on a morning after the miracle of rain. That day it was overprinted on black ink stories of hard times beginning to soften to good, of a panhandle family once torn asunder and now reunited in the relative plenty of California, of the dawning hope of what was being termed a New Deal.

"It was Christmas Eve, turning cold, and I didn't have a penny to my name when out of the heavens arrived not only food and shelter, but an income and a purpose to fill my life."

Jewel told me all this a couple of Christmases after the big golf match. Christmas had always been an introspective time for her, a time when her thoughts turned away from others, the only time that her expansive personality was insufficient to fill her many parental roles. Even at age ten, I wondered why it had long been up to me to play Santa. About the time I entered high school, I finally asked her.

"I was smart enough to keep quiet about the baby," she said. "The Mother Superior would find out about that sooner or later, but in the meantime, I would be a teacher. And when March came for me, I would still be a teacher. Perhaps I was afflicted with my father's talent to instill, but I would not disseminate blindness as my father had—I would spread light."

Growing up in Del Rio, Jewel's Spanish was second natural. While she taught the nuns to speak English, she also increased their knowledge of Spanish grammar, and taught them to read and write in both languages. By the time Jewel could no longer hide her condition, not only would it have been inhuman to turn her out, it would have been impossible. The convent had begun to depend upon her.

Besides, Jewel told herself, she would only be there until March came for her. Roscoe would take the letter to March, and

March would come. It wouldn't be long. He was bound to come. But Jewel grew larger and larger, and March did not arrive.

In despair, Jewel decided that she would wait for the baby's arrival, then notify him one last time. She felt that if the baby was born much more than nine months after she met Roscoe at the Wing Ding, that if she could keep that baby inside her by sheer will until enough weeks and months had passed, then it couldn't possibly be Roscoe's child, and could belong only to March. It was a matter of inner strength, of refusing to let go. And it was a feat she accomplished with ease.

"I had some small contractions and a couple of false alarms," Jewel told me. "But I made it past nine months, and I was sure that everything would be okay.

"The convent had a musty library—just a dim room with stacks of old books. Every day I'd sort through some of the mess and try to get things organized. Books in English I'd arrange on one wall, books in Spanish on another. One morning I came across a medical book in Spanish. The true measure of a pregnancy, it said, was not nine months, but forty weeks.

"Feeling faint, I leaned back against the wall, and dropped the book to the floor. A spasm pulled at my stomach. Then another. 'No!' I cried out. 'Not yet! It's too soon.'

"Unable to walk, I laid down on the floor. Alone, in a room no bigger than a closet, I fought to keep your mother inside of me. Sister Elena found me—I don't know how long it had been—and they put me in bed for the baby's arrival. They told me to push, and I pulled. They told me to pant, and I held my breath. They told me to relax against the contractions, and I fought them with every ounce of strength. I *knew* that it was March's baby, and only I could prove it."

It was a battle of nature against will, a battle that two weeks later still had Jewel refusing to push until she could refuse no more, until a baby girl forced her way into the world as March's rightful child.

And that was my mother, Martha Anne Hemphill, who, no matter how much affection and reassurance she was given in her life, never felt wanted in her home or in this world at all. Sometimes on the coldest nights of winter, even after all these years, I listen to the January winds howling through the bare trees outside my window, and I wonder what became of her.

SNEAK AROUND IN THE bushes eavesdropping on any regular golf foursome and you'll hear them talking about the random breaks of the game. If one golfer lips out eight putts in a row, his partners and opponents will just shrug and say the cup's too small (in fact, the ball lips out because the cup is round and not square). If the weird breaks and unlikely bounces start rearing their ugly heads to another in the group, it's explained that the unlucky golfer didn't go to church on Sunday (of course he went to church, he played golf). And hitting one tree or barely catching the lip of just one trap is a sure invitation to repeat the disaster over and over again.

"The golf gods just weren't with you today," console the playing partners. "You must have pissed off somebody upstairs."

If you stop to think about it, these players are describing the true nature of the game. Golf is more religion than sport, a religion with a very tiny and unforgiving goal: perfection. And as in some groovy Eastern religion, the golf gods have a habit of rewarding the believer who approaches that perfection with a yin/yang philosophy of both diligence and indifference. Work your tail off to learn each and every shot that may confront you, but try not to give a hoot about any of them. The way to golf in the groove is to not worry about the ball going in the hole, but rather to just get in the groove and stay there—the golf gods allowing, that is.

When I was caddying for Sandy at one of the Texas regional qualifiers, he started off by telling me he'd been hitting the ball great, never better.

"I don't know," he said, half talking to himself. "I been in the groove for weeks. Every shot seems sweet and pure. I can feel it, twenty-four hours a day. I can feel it at breakfast, I can feel it at dinner. I can feel it in my sleep."

"That's super!" I told him.

"Yeah, I guess. Except . . ."

"Except what?"

"Now I don't feel it. I woke up this morning and it was gone. I can still chip and putt. I been out here practicing for hours and I can still hit the shots, but I can't *feel* it anymore."

He was right. It was gone. Poof! Vanished like a genie after the third wish. And there was nothing Sandy could do about it. He was damned lucky to beat some yo-yo with a swing worse than my own.

"God, I want it back," Sandy said to me after the match. "I want it back so bad!"

What was the problem? Was he trying too hard? Had he offended the golf gods? Or did he just have too many sticks in his bag? That was March's theory.

"The problem with golf," March told me, "is you got too many tools. You give a carpenter fourteen hammers all different weights and lengths, and I guarantee he'll come home with his thumb beat to a bloody pulp. We don't half know how hard this game is. Fact is, we're lucky to come back alive."

The fact is, golf is a fickle game: alive, but only in myth; marvelous, but only in theory; generous, but rarely in practice. I don't know why we curse and pray to the gods of golf. Do they live only in our minds, or are we, the mortal golfers, the products of their invention? No one really knows, of course, because it's a question meant for keener minds than those who take up sticks and balls as an unwitting form of worship.

And speaking of those without keen minds, Beast had been casually rewarded one of the worst breaks in golf. His approach shot to the seventh green backed all the way from the hole to the front edge of the green, and finally came to rest against the first cut or ridge between the short grass and the longer fringe. In such a case it's nigh on impossible to get the flat blade of the putter onto the full face of the ball. Either the flat iron hangs up in the thick grass behind the ball, or it sweeps over the grass and tops the ball. To compound matters, there was a twisting, double-helix break between his ball and the hole. For once I was glad he didn't ask me for assistance in reading the putt. Instead, he asked for his wedge.

I'd long heard of a Texas sand wedge—using a putter from a sand trap—but the other way around—a wedge from the green—that *must be* what an overly proud Texan would call an Oklahoma putter. Beast, with an already difficult putt, hoped to sweep the sole of the club over the deep fringe and square into the middle of the ball, which was just peeking at him over the lip of grass. Getting the ball near the hole would have been quite a feat. Knocking it dead in the heart for a birdie would have been a true miracle. And that's exactly what Beast did. Some days chicken; some days feathers.

"Hot damn!" said Roscoe. "My animal came to play!"

"One up," said Fromholz. "One up, two to go."

The golf gods had certainly come down upon Sandy, who sunk his head into his hands as if the whole match was over. But you wouldn't have known it by March. Having rejoined the game, he tried to recharge Sandy's spirit with another song.

"Oh, there's free beer tomorrow,
But there's heartache today!
Now we're filled with sorrow,
But tomorrow we won't pay!"

In wonder, Sandy turned to look at his older partner, whose boundless optimism seemed incapable of giving in.

"It ain't over till it's over," March told him with a wink.

Knowing that in golf one never abandons ship, Sandy nodded his head in reply.

Beast, meanwhile, walked cockily up to the hole, stuck his wedge into it, and popped the ball straight up into the air. Instead of catching the ball in his hand, though, he bounced it several more times on the flat blade of the wedge.

"That's quite a little circus trick, Bobo," said March. "Bet you can't bounce it fifty times without missing."

Beast quickly caught the ball and turned to March. "How much?"

"Fifty bucks!" said March. "A buck a bounce."

"Done," said Beast, with a loud crack of his knuckles. Holding the wedge just below the grip, he began to bounce the ball up and down as easily as if it were on a tennis racquet.

Everyone paused to watch. Around bounce forty, he nearly missed and the ball went off at a sharp angle, but Beast deftly extended the club and brought the errant orb back into its vertical hop.

"Forty-eight, forty-nine, fifty!" counted Beast and Fromholz.

"Pay up, doofus!" added Beast. "You owe me half a c-note."

March already had in his hand the engraving of Grant looking green.

"Tell you what, big man," March told him. "I'll bet you can't do five hundred bounces for five hundred bucks!"

"Money from home," said Beast, turning toward the eighth tee. "Somebody help me count."

And with Fromholz trailing behind, Beast strolled casually across the green, whistling off-key as he bounced the ball on the wedge over and over and over.

In addition to playing both left- and right-handed, links hustler Titanic Thompson had quite a few other interesting golf bets: that he could chip a ball into a hat from thirty feet; balance a driver, a golf ball and a tee on his nose; or hit a drive half a mile at the place of his choosing (he chose a frozen lake).

My favorite of his short cons, like Beast's trick wedge bounce, wasn't really a golf bet at all; it just took place on a golf course with golf equipment. Having reamed his suckers right-handed, left-handed, one-handed, and possibly even no-handed (he could putt with his foot), Ti would generally say he felt sorry for his opponents and suggest some wild and wonderful wager so they could win their money back.

Back at the car, having already untied his golf shoes, he'd take out his putter and hold it by each end. Then he'd wager that he could jump out of his shoes, pass his bare feet over the putter held horizontally in his hands, and land his feet back in his golf shoes. This was clearly impossible, and I doubt that anyone ever declined the wager.

It was said that Ti won a quarter of a million dollars a year for fifty years with his original short cons. And I wouldn't be surprised if half of it was with that single impossible feat, a stunt that he could accomplish each and every time. How did he do it? He was a natural athlete, he practiced for hours a day—after all, hustling was his job—and what the heck, maybe the golf gods were just on his side.

BEAST WAS ALREADY ON the four hundredth bounce when he arrived at the eighth tee. Fromholz, still counting, eased up next to me.

"This guy . . ." Fromholz said to me softly. "Four-o-eight, four-o-nine . . . This guy pisses me off! Four-eleven, four-twelve . . ."

"You missed one!" yelled Beast, still bouncing. "You started jabbering and you missed one!"

"No I didn't," answered Fromholz, skipping several more.

"Yes you did, you missed one!" Beast insisted.

"Are you sure?" asked Fromholz, no longer counting at all.

"Damn right I am!"

"Okay. You ought to know. Four-thirteen, four-*fifteen*," skipping forward one bounce in correction, by then having missed at least twenty others.

I expected Beast to be pissed about Fromholz's tactics or for March to jump in there and distract Beast himself, but the fact was March had made a bad bet. As if to prove it, while the ball bounced toward five hundred, Beast explained to us that he had learned the trick by picking up balls on his dad's range: bucket in one hand, wedge in the other, he'd slip the blade of the wedge under a ball, pop it into the air and bounce it into the bucket. If he had to walk to the next ball, he continued bouncing the first one until it was time to lift the next.

"It's been a few years," boasted Beast, "but I've done at least a million bounces!"

"Four-ninety-nine, five hundred," Fromholz concluded.

"Too bad I didn't get a buck from some sucker for every one of them. Come on, March, pay up! You owe me five hundred!"

"Yes I do," agreed March. "But you'll have to be patient 'cause my money's in the car."

"It better be!" crowed Beast. "I don't like a guy who welshes on a bet!"

"Nobody does," added Fromholz, shutting the Beast up cold.

Jewel slid up next to March and took his hand. I'm not sure if it was a sign of affection or if she was just checking his pulse.

"Nice bet, William," she said. "Are you still going to have a little money left when this thing's over? Three don't live too easily on a teacher's salary."

"Well, Jewel," piped March, "let's don't worry about that. When life deals you lemons, you just gotta make whiskey sours."

This put a frown on Jewel's face. Now that she had March, the challenge was not only to keep him alive but also to mold him into some sort of respectable head of a household. Her prospects for accomplishing the latter, I viewed as slim. Roscoe, on the other hand, just wanted to get the whole thing over with so he wouldn't ever again have to watch Jewel and March talking soft and sweet.

"Beast! Your shot!" he barked.

Beast asked for a six-iron and stepped onto the tee. As soon as he moved into his stance I could tell something was wrong. He was gripping the club kind of funny and there was a slight tremor to the clubhead, as if we were in a small earthquake.

Being a seasoned veteran, Beast backed away. He cracked his

knuckles loudly, then regripped the club and stepped back up. If anything, the shaking had grown worse. I saw him tighten his grip to a choke-hold, a terrible mistake common to duffers and high handicappers. As Roscoe might have put it, the true golf grip is no tighter than a prostitute handling a teenage boy.

"What's wrong?" asked Roscoe. There was a note of panic in his voice as Beast backed away again.

"I don't know," said the big man. "My right hand feels screwy. I guess I was gripping my wedge and bouncing that ball too long at a time."

March, like the March of old, was grinning from ear to ear, winking at Sandy and making goo-goo eyes at Jewel, all at the same time.

"My partner the dumb-butt!" said Roscoe. "I swear, if we wuz to shove a bowling ball in your brain, it'd bounce around like a BB in a boxcar! Hell, if you wait much longer, Fromholz'll probably penalize you for slow play. He don't really seem to care much for you anyways, so you better swallow your medicine and hit it."

Beast was so shaken that he sculled the top half of the ball and it flew like a wounded quail only halfway to the green. To his credit, I must add that Beast had learned one thing: he didn't break his club. There was one hole left in the match. Instead he squinted his red eyes toward a white-tailed deer that his shot had flushed out of a shady midday bed in the left rough. Bambi had trotted out into the middle of the fairway, where she stood broadsided looking at us.

Beast tossed down a second ball. Puzzled at what he was doing, the rest of us watched as he again moved into his stance—his hands quivering with rage this time, as he shifted them forward, effectively turning the six-iron into a two- or three-iron of destruction.

I don't know whether he was trying to further prove his idiocy or his golf prowess, but before anyone could stop him, he took a flat, short backswing and smashed the second ball at the unsuspecting doe. The ball whistled through the air and slammed into her hindquarters with a sickening thud that sounded like a hollow-point bullet finding flesh. The deer actually went down for a moment, then leapt to her feet and sped off limping on three legs.

"Got her!" yelled Beast. "How's that for a shot?"

His gloating gaze panned over our wide-eyed horror and came to rest on Fromholz, now striding quickly toward him. Beast made as if to defend himself with the six-iron, but Fromholz deftly took it away from him and laid the big man out on the ground with some sort of jujitsu or karate maneuver. Then Fromholz raised the club above Beast's head as if to strike him dead between the eyes.

"How'd you like to get hit with a six-iron, you steaming sack of white-trash defecation? You a wimp! You know that? You some kind of wimp and a bum and an egg-sucking half-breed, diseased mongrel that ought to be sent to the glue factory in a little box. If you ever do that again, I'll kill you twice and enjoy it both times. What do you say, pussy, should I hit you?"

"I been hit," stuttered Beast, almost in tears. "M-my old man hit me, lots of times."

This was a good tactic. Our hearts softened almost immediately. Fromholz, his damaged eye about to pop out of his face, suddenly looked more like an animal than the cowering Beast. The ref even felt it himself.

"Sorry, Hoss!" Fromholz said, grabbing the big man by the forearm and helping him to his feet. "When you were a kid, huh? Man, that's tough. How old were you?"

"Thirteen," said Beast. But then he realized that this figure didn't seem that young for such a big guy. "Thirteen," he corrected himself, "the last time."

I don't really know what moved him to tell us this story. I don't even know if it was true. He might have been trying to escape Fromholz's anger, but just maybe he really was a great big scared and lonely galoot, haunted by his past and terrified of falling back into that hardscrabble life.

"When the driving range got real crowded on holidays and stuff," Beast began, "we'd run out of balls and my old man would make me pick 'em up while people was still hitting 'em. So he used to dress me up in this stupid padded jacket and football helmet, and I'd walk around out there with a bucket and a club picking up balls. So one day I'm out there with my four-iron and the people on the tee are laughing at my football helmet and they're hitting balls at me. It's not too bad to get hit in the jacket, but this one guy—I seen him—he beans me in the football helmet twice in a row. I mean he rang my bell. I got so mad I dumped all the balls down and started hitting 'em back at the tee. It was great! All them golfers yelling and screaming and running for cover. Man, they were getting in their cars and peeling out of the parking lot, and then I sorta accidentally hit one guy in the face with a ball. It wasn't even the same guy that had been hitting at me. It was just some guy and he got hurt bad. The ambulance came and took him away. Afterwards, my old man beat the crap out of me."

When Beast finished the story, there was a long, uncomfortable silence.

"Pop mighta killed me," Beast concluded, "if I hadn't of knocked him out with a shovel."

As he finished the story, his downcast eyes lifted long enough to check the reactions on our faces. And just as he turned his own face back to the ground, I thought I saw the slightest smile.

"Very interesting, Mr. Larsen," said March. "A good example of how cruel and unfair life can be." Then almost as an afterthought he said, "Fromholz. Lemme ask you again, how'd you lose that eye?"

We all turned to Fromholz.

"I was hit in the face with a golf ball," he answered. "On a driving range."

Beast shrunk back—rather ashen-faced I thought—and Sandy stepped to the tee box.

THE FIRST TIME I saw Sandy hit the flagstick with his tee shot, I thought it the most amazing thing I'd ever witnessed and I gushed like a fool. Sandy had to remind me that not only had the ball not gone in, but with the bounce off the metal post, it had actually ended up farther away than if it had just bit into the grass.

In subsequent rounds I managed to control my enthusiasm as he continued on a long string of almost aces. Once he nearly made two holes-in-one in the same round. It was incredible the way he was bouncing them off and lipping them out and hopping them over. And these near miracles didn't seem like good luck at all. To me, it seemed like every one of those shots should have gone in. They looked perfect; why shouldn't they drop?

Sandy explained to me that scoring well doesn't require many great shots. Even for a duffer, one good shot is all you need to make a bogey on a par four. Two good shots—say a nice drive and a good putt to go with it—will usually earn you a par. The problem with birdie is that it usually takes three good shots in a row, a feat beyond most golfers whose handicaps or ratings as excellent, fair, or pitiful players are generally just an indication of how consistently they strike the ball.

"You're not as good as your best shot," Sandy told me. "You're only as good as your worst."

And since Sandy didn't have a bad shot in the bag, he was darn good. I knew it was only a matter of time before he fired one of those middle-irons at the flag and left all the bad luck and crummy bounces behind him by sailing or bouncing or rolling one into the hole. All he had to do was forget that he was spooked and quit concentrating on the little things that didn't mean anything, like the fox running in front of the car or his history of losing to Beast. None of it would mean anything to Sandy's game as soon as it didn't mean anything to Sandy.

As he stepped onto the eighth tee, Sandy knew he had to win the hole or lose the match. He lofted a pinch of grass into the air to test the wind, and in the stillness of the coming midday, it fell straight down below his hand. Then he tossed aside one of the two clubs in his hand—I think it was the six-iron—and stepped up to the snowy-white hundred-compression Titleist he'd just taken out of a new sleeve of three.

In unison with Sandy, my right hand tightened gently, as if I too were gripping the club. To hide the involuntary action, I slipped my hand into my pocket and discovered something cool and hard and marvelous. It was March's moon rock. My fingers closed into a tight fist around the magic stone, and I could almost feel it begin to glow as I wished: "Go in! Go in!"

"Go in!" I silently and fervently urged as Sandy took the club back, turning then tilting his shoulders, reversing on the down-swing, tilting then turning back, and carving across the lower inside corner of the ball so that it arced in a high-drawn trace of light to the green.

I never ceased to marvel at how Sandy could divide the back face of the ball into quarters, almost like slicing a cherry pie. He'd adjust his swing trajectory and move the clubhead into the quarter of his intention, hitting either a low-cut fade, a high fade, a high hook or a low draw to suit his needs. It was as if the land had been tailored to the swing rather than vice versa, golf mechanics and shotmaking at their finest, and Sandy used this skill at will. He used the high shots and the following breeze to stretch a seven-iron to a hundred and seventy yards, as he was doing here, or the easy-swinging low shots with a minimum of spin that could bore a hole into an onslaught of wind.

The greatest marvel of all was that he never knew how impossibly difficult these feats were. Sandy seemed to think that all good golfers understood and mastered such mechanics. And thus he underestimated his own abilities by half, shutting the door on the greatest tool of all: confidence.

"Don't move, hole," said Fromholz.

"Go in!" I silently begged the gods of golf, my hand squeezing the moon rock tightly. "Go in, go in!"

The ball hit two feet short of the hole and hopped directly into the cup. It was in the hole. There was no doubt about it, but still I kept wishing. "Go in. Go in." It had dived in there so hot, I figured it might be thinking about hopping out again.

There was a long silence, broken by March.

"I'll be damned! An ace in one!"

"With one hole to go," translated Fromholz. "This match is all even."

Before Sandy shook our offered hands of congratulation, he bent over to replace his divot, mopping the tears from his eyes so we wouldn't see them.

"BIG GIRLS DON'T CRY," the school bullies taunted me as they twisted my spine. But I cried anyway. It took me a long time to learn there's no shame in yesterday's tears, only a salty aftertaste. That's part of what makes it possible to write about the way things were. But the meaning of this story that has so long haunted me is equally related to the way things are. And that is not so easy.

Freelance advertising writer. I dislike advertising in general but find that I'm pretty good at writing it, so instead of working for one firm and being assigned whatever stupid accounts please them, I basically work for no one. The only way I get on an account is to find a product I like, come up with a snappy way to sell it, and then pitch myself, and my idea, to the agency in charge. The agency then has three choices. Number one, they can kick me out on my ass because they think I'm an idiot. Number two, they can steal my idea because they think I'm a fool. Number three, they can buy my idea and hire me to see it through because they think I'm a genius. The infrequency of the latter leaves me a lot of time for golf.

Don't think this commercial independence in any way makes me an advertising elitist. My most successful gig to date has been boosting a marginal office products company into a hit regional chain, a feat accomplished through the oldest sham in the book: sex. I wrote a spot that featured a gorgeous long-legged secretary and a handsome upper-management male boss, both shopping and flirting at the office store where the beautiful people shop. And for a follow-up spot, I made the secretary a gentle but bluff young man and the boss a sexy business-suited woman. It's low rent, but it works.

That's why, when I got a chance to pitch to golf's most classic clubmaker—the Ben Hogan Company of Fort Worth, Texas—my mind immediately went to sex. This may sound like a leap of logic and a violation of faith, but sex has rarely been used to sell golf or golf clubs. Unable to come up with anything better, I was desperate enough to think it would work.

For once, the agency actually called me. They wanted a thirty-second spot and they wanted it to pop out of the screen. Something new and wonderful that would make people jump their lard butts up off their sofas and run out and buy a full set of Ben Hogan golf clubs for a sum of money roughly equal to the national debt of Argentina. Even though all golfers want to hit the ball farther, I knew we couldn't use that tack. Longer is the claim used to sell golf balls, not golf clubs.

Longer, no. Sexier, yes. Why sell only golf balls when you can make a commercial that will sell anything? The spot I pitched to the agency had a comely young woman watching a classically sculpted male golfer eyeing his target and grabbing a Hogan five-iron (in close-up, of course). Addressing the ball with his perfect stance, his fans in the background (including the babe) watch his fluid swing with long, arcing extension and a follow-through that slaps him on the ass in a manner with which we are all now familiar. We see the woman's little thrill at the slap on the ass and her disappointment as the ball lands ten feet past the pin. Then suddenly the ball spins furiously back toward the hole and drops in. The woman gasps with passion and, as the young stud kisses the club, we see the brand name again in close-up: "Hogan."

The agency sent me packing.

The next day I was riding Amtrak's Texas Eagle to Fort Worth. I had been given the opportunity to present the idea to the man himself, Mr. Ben Hogan, winner of four U.S. Opens, perhaps the greatest ball striker who ever lived, and the designer of the club with which Sandy had made that timely hole-in-one.

During the trip, I kept thinking about how Hogan was famed during his years on Tour for being a very quiet man. Several golfers reported that the only two words Hogan said during an entire round were while putting, and those of course were: "You're away."

Having been wined and dined the evening before by the potential producer and director of the commercial (both of whom needed the job as much as I did), I was convinced that my idea was flawless. "Nobel and Pulitzer prize material" was how they put it.

Still, the idea of meeting Hogan terrified me, and I walked into the Hogan complex with no more confidence than I had possessed at age thirteen when I walked into my first office building to see March. Again I was ushered down a hallway lined with golf photos—none featuring horses, I was disappointed to note—and steered through an imposing door to meet the man himself. If my mouth hadn't been so dry, I'd have peed my pants.

I sat down across from his desk, mesmerized by his lined face, reflective of a life's dedication to a single passion. I could see his eyes, flecked with the various victories and defeats of his life in golf. And it seemed to me that the darkness around them was just the shadow of the Greyhound bus that smashed head-on into his car on a lonely West Texas highway so many years before, mangling his body and threatening his ability either to play golf or to ever walk again. And the eyelids, blinking just a little more often than you'd expect, seemed no more than the constant memory of the failed nerve yips that had rendered him unable to putt even two-footers. And yet he had risen above it all, as a champion golfer, as one of the most respected names in the history of the game, and as the designer and manufacturer of a line of golf equipment that his customers have been known to take to their graves.

Suddenly I realized my idea was all wrong. I was a fool for thinking golf clubs were just another interchangeable product like underarm deodorant or Odor Eaters for shoes. Golf isn't sex. Golf is passion, the passion of graceful fools and awkward poets and those who refuse to lay down forever without first dreaming of fleeting perfection. I cleared my throat loudly and, failing to hack up any kind of alternate plan, said nothing.

Hogan looked me up and down, didn't seem too impressed by what he saw, and uttered two words: "You're away."

I think he was kidding me, but I gathered that it was my time to pitch. I bit my lip and told him that the idea I'd tossed at the agency was the infantile fantasy of a man overcome by temporary insanity, that it had absolutely nothing to do with his company, and could have been used to sell anything from pork rinds to porch swings. Then I hung my head in shame that I'd wasted his time.

This increased Mr. Hogan's word usage to three. "Good for you."

We spent the rest of the day touring his operation, watching the hand-lathing of persimmon clubheads, the hosels being readied for the insertion of high-tech shafts, and finally the finished clubs coming off the line. We passed the golden-lit hours of the early evening reviewing scrapbooks in the library that practically breathed of his many Tour wins, especially the near Grand Slam of 1953 when the British Open, U.S. Open and Masters all fell to the attack of his relentless course management, and only the PGA escaped the grasp of his genius.

That night I awoke in a start, picked up a pen and paper from beside the hotel bed, and hurriedly scribbled down the dream that had been playing in a loop inside my head.

Traveling shot: The camera flies lovingly over the misty moors of Scotland. A hundred bagpipers are seen in the distance. We hear the emotional lilting strains of "Amazing Grace." As the camera glides over a little hillock we see two men alone in an expanse of gorse and green. Close-up: A young Scotsman of the 1930s is dressed in the traditional golfing plus-fours of his day. He makes a breathtaking pass at his ball. Backlit by the shimmering waters of the Firth of Forth, the ball soars above the mist and bounds close to the hole on the seventh green at St. Andrews.

Near the Scottish golfer in the fairway is the young Ben Hogan, the initials *BH* on his sweater. He selects a club and swings crisply. The ball sails low and draws in on the flag, landing short and bounding tight inside his opponent's ball. Close-up: The young Scot extends a hand of congratulation to the young Texan. Both smile. Cut to: company logo: "Hogan—Timeless Perfection."

That's it. No babes, no bouncing breasts, no frenzied fans, no holes-in-one. We made the spot. It ran for sixty seconds instead of thirty, and sales went up sixteen percent in one month. I hoped Mr. Hogan would call to say "Good work," but he never did.

As Sandy strode down the eighth fairway to remove his ball from the hole, he might have been twenty-year-old amateur golfer and former caddie Francis Ouimet who defeated British pros

Harry Vardon and Ted Ray in a play-off for the 1913 U.S. Open. Or Bobby Jones triumphantly strolling down the home hole at the Old Course in St. Andrews, moments before being swarmed by thousands of Scottish fans upon winning his second British Open in 1927. He could even have been his own hero, Ben Hogan, winning the 1950 U.S. Open only a year after his bus accident, when the doctors said he'd never play again. Or he might have been a thousand other triumphant golfers on a thousand other splendorous days. For Sandy was living the supreme moment of the game—temporarily victorious before facing the next hole, or the next match, or the next tournament.

Had Sandy not been dressed as a golfer, I could just as easily have seen Babe Ruth rounding the bases in the 1926 World Series after pointing over the center-field wall, claiming in advance one of his 714 major league home runs. This one was for an eleven-year-old fan, the critically ill Johnny Sylvester, who despite the doctor's prognosis recovered and lived to return the favor years later by holding the great one's hand on Ruth's own deathbed. Or he might have been Jesse Owens climbing the steps of glory again and again, weighted by Olympic gold and lightened by the proof of his accomplishments in Nazi Berlin. But Sandy Bates was my friend and teacher and a hero who, like all heroes, would be remembered in some quarter of heaven for his fleeting but indelible moment of glory while tromping his own hallowed grounds.

Stepping across the green without putter or hesitation, Sandy removed the flag, bent so that his hand disappeared into the earth, and picked the magic ball out of the hole. We watched him silently: partners, opponents, spectator and judge, and deep in our own hearts, each of us was extremely jealous.

WHETHER YOU PLAY NINE, eighteen or twenty-seven holes, a golf course needs a tough finishing hole to weed out the losers. That's especially true for a nine-hole course where you may play the ninth from one to five times a day, depending on how die-hard a golfer you are. On a hot day, or when you're just sneaking in a little practice round before work, you may be quitting after playing only nine. If you've escaped more worldly worries, you may be passing number nine every couple of hours until it gets too dark to find your ball. You can play the first nine from the white tees, the second from the blues, and the third from the tips. If you're a big enough golf-nut to go for thirty-six or forty-five holes, you can always experiment with a nine-hole scramble or a one-club competition (a five-iron is a good choice).

Perhaps to discourage too much of this repetitive, course-crowding play, the Pedernales layout took the concept of a tough finishing hole one step further. So difficult was number nine that you'd be happy just to have survived the hole and delighted to put the clubs back in your trunk. From the back tees, it was four hundred and twenty-five yards long, with a big dogleg to the left, and a long iron from the fairway to a green elevated almost to heaven. The hole couldn't have been better suited for deciding a big match.

Pumped with adrenaline and covered with goose bumps at having just accomplished the ultimate feat in golf, Sandy stepped quickly to the tee. Taking the club back faster than usual, he snap-hooked his tee shot deep into the left rough. We were stunned. With the match even and the momentum in his favor, he'd choked like a rookie.

"Sorry, March," Sandy mumbled as he slunk back.

While Sandy hit, March had rested his hand—and most of his weight—somewhat affectionately on my shoulder. Though their team's outlook had recovered somewhat (till now), March hadn't recovered at all. His color had returned, but only in splotches, and he'd hit just one shot since the fisticuffs with Roscoe, and it hadn't been for beans. Now the pressure was weighing heavily on him. It took him a long time to get his tee into the ground, and as he prepared to swing, the ball fell off the tee. He bent to replace it, then backed away taking short, shallow breaths, as if he could cool himself like a panting hound.

"Roscoe," he gasped. "You hit. I got to catch my breath."

Roscoe didn't challenge the request, didn't call for a ruling about hitting in turn, didn't make a smart-ass remark. He just stepped up and hit his shot. It was the only nice thing I ever saw him do.

"Beast," Roscoe said to the big man. "Now you forget about that lucky hole-in-one thing and hit it good."

"Hole-in-one?" Beast asked as if he hadn't seen it. "Shit, that's old news, just like that birdie I made on seven. It don't matter anymore. The guys that win here take home the big bucks and everybody else sucks on the hind teat."

Why Beast had started with any woods at all was a mystery to me. He sure didn't need them. His one-iron shot was as certain as the day and just as long, sending the ball maybe two hundred and forty yards as the crow flies. What with cutting forty yards off the corner, his ball was soon nestled tight against the bottom of the hill, looking directly up at the green.

Now more than ever, it was up to March. Jewel gave him her blessing in the form of a kiss on his cheek. Then he looked at me for a long time, as if he was trying to memorize my face. With a final wink he stepped back onto the tee.

He had no energy for a practice swing or even for a simple waggle of the clubhead. Though he was saving all his available energy for the task at hand, it was easy to see that the well had gone dry. Shakily, he started the clubhead back, but already he was sinking, calling for his medicine as he hit the ground.

I ran to Roscoe's cart and reached for the pocket on March's bag where I'd put the medicine. The zipper was open partway but I didn't think anything of it; I just yanked it the rest of the way down and started pulling stuff out: a white handkerchief, an "Old Timer" pocket knife, rusted spare cleats, pencils . . . and nothing else. The medicine wasn't there.

"Billy!" called Jewel. "Hurry! Please hurry!"

Frantically I searched again through the stuff I'd dumped out, through the empty pocket, and through the other pockets too. There was no medicine.

"It's not here!" I cried. "It's not in the pocket where I put it!"

Sandy shoved me aside and began to search himself. That's when it dawned on me about the zipper being down. I wouldn't have done that, would I? Left the zipper down and let March's medicine bounce out?

God, please! Please don't tell me I've lost March's medicine.

I ran to him to see if he was better, but the fact was, he really didn't need the medicine at all. Not anymore. His head was in Jewel's lap and she was fanning his face, trying to give him a little air. He held up his hand toward me and I put mine in his. His palm felt tough and wonderful, but I knew that he was dying, and I began to cry.

"The pills aren't there," I told him, trying to hold back my sobs.

The last trump had been played and the look on March's face was wry. Lifting up his head, he gazed to the distant hills, then back to me.

"It's okay," he said. "It's a nice spot to die."

I remember he told me I shouldn't cry.

Roscoe hobbled over and looked down at his former partner.

"Looks like you drilled your last hole, March. Well, least you got clean living on your side."

March removed his right hand from mine and held it slowly out to Roscoe. They shook, despite everything, companions in the end. Then March pulled me toward him. He couldn't talk so well, but he had a big smile on his face because Jewel's tears were streaming off her cheeks and falling onto him like a small rainstorm. He pulled me down close, inches from his lips, and whispered something into my ear, whispered so softly that I couldn't even tell for certain what he said. It was two words, I thought: "Last green."

Just then Fromholz returned with some water and pulled me away.

I stepped back in shock. Last green? Of course it's the last green. What was that supposed to mean? *His* last green? *Our* last green? March was dying, Sandy was losing, and I was more confused than ever.

My hand was warm where March had held it. I thrust it into my pocket and found my magic moon rock waiting for me there. "All you have to do is wish," March had told me. I grasped the rock and squeezed with all my might, wishing my heart out: "Don't die! Don't die, March! Please don't die!"

March opened his eyes again and found the strength to speak.

"Jewel, you were the best thing in my life. I'm sorry I let you down."

Then his eyes closed slowly. Jewel looked up at us accusingly.

"Don't die!" I wished. "March, please don't die."

But it wasn't enough.

After a moment, Fromholz knelt down beside the lost lovers and very professionally put a finger to a vein behind March's ear.

"Well, fellas," he told us. "Ol' March here is just deader'n hell."

My breath left me in a single rush. Unable to think or even see, I took the moon rock out of my pocket and, through my tears, blindly tried to focus on it. The rock was a fraud, a phony, a false and hateful kind of worthless trickery that pretended responsibility for Sandy's ace, and then just as inertly, it allowed March to die. It was fake magic, just like March was a fake father and an even bigger fake of a grandfather: now you see him; now you don't! I hurled the heavy rock off the hilltop as hard as I could. It sailed with a sudden breeze and far from my sight it struck the earth for the second time in a millennium.

Jewel was still kneeling at March's side, singing some little Mexican song for him. Roscoe leaned down and took her arm lightly.

"Come on, Jewel, let's go. There's nothing you can do now."

Jewel looked up at him coldly. "Roscoe Fowler, if I ever see you again," she hissed, "I'll cut out your heart with a rusty letter opener and serve it to you with a side of human decency! Now get away from me!"

Roscoe pulled back and walked toward his cart. "Crazy bitch!" he muttered.

I pulled the driver from March's hands, ready to plant it in the soft spot in the back of Roscoe's skull, but Sandy stopped me.

"Let's finish the match," he said. "That's what March would have wanted."

The driver was in my hands and March's ball was still on the tee as Roscoe, Beast and Sandy started down the fairway. I aimed over their heads and struck the ball a mighty blow. It soared into the sky, and as it started to fall, I thought I saw some glimmer of light, some essence of March's heart and soul, break away and fly up to heaven.

Like most boys, I once had a dog; the gentlest little half golden retriever–half Border collie you could ever imagine. She wasn't quite as dumb or stick crazy as most retrievers, and she'd missed out on some of her Border collie work ethic, but she loved to curl back her lips and nip at my heels as if I were a sheep out of line. She also loved to fetch my chip shots and drop them right where I could hit them again, without having to adjust my stance forward or back, and then she'd chase the ball again. A dedicated retriever of golf balls is one that doesn't mind if you blade it thin, shank it thick, or top it dumb, but brings them all back along with the occasional good shots.

One day the dreaded "S" word reared its ugly head and I shanked a little wedge shot that skidded across the practice green at Santa Fe Park and bounced out onto Beauregard Avenue. I yelled for her to stop, but a golden always gets her ball.

I don't remember the car that hit her or the driver who stopped to try to help. I just remember that sweet, beautiful dog as she came limping and dragging back toward me in horrid shock: screaming for me to make it better, crying for me to stop the pain, howling in lack of understanding of what had happened. How could life have been so wonderful one minute, chasing balls for her buddy, and so filled with pain the next?

It seemed to take her a long time to die. I buried her in the unkempt edges of the park, down by the river where she once caught a rabbit and carried it proudly back to show me. It was the only time I ever hit her—how dare she kill such a little creature! When I struck her she dropped the rabbit, and she'd been holding it so gently in her teeth that the bunny ran away unharmed. I've never quit regretting hitting that dog, not yet anyway. And the thing it taught me is that regret has the ability to change the past not one iota.

"A high rate of regret," March had told me.

What I gathered he meant was that his field was full, there was no more fertile imagination in which to sow weeds and stickers, only a field too overgrown to plow. And now March would have to plow no more. From here on in it would be nothing but soft greens and good bounces, an unbroken string of pars and birdies, and a very low rate of regret.

FROM THAT LAST, LONELY fairway I looked back over my shoulder and saw that Jewel was still kneeling next to March. Her hair was in disarray, the careful bun fallen and her tresses down about her face like a veil. It was hot out in the sun and she had the two of them in the shade of her little parasol.

She'll be okay, I thought. We'll leave her alone while we finish, and then go back to help.

Between the tee and the fairway I'd almost cried out in despair at the thought that my carelessness might have killed March. I remembered putting the medicine in the pocket of the bag and I thought I remembered zipping it up, but there was no sound to go with the memory of the zipper closing. We'd moved March's bag to Roscoe's cart just after that. Maybe the medicine fell out when the bag was tipped. . . .

And then it came to me. In a Texas flood of terrible understanding it washed my guilt away. Roscoe had been screwing around with March's bag. I hadn't left the zipper down, Roscoe had. Roscoe had stolen the medicine from March's bag, and either not managed to close the zipper or left it down on purpose so that it would look like an accident.

Roscoe was climbing out of his cart nearby. Even in the heat he looked cool and composed.

Cold-blooded, I thought. Isn't that what it's called? Cold-blooded murder.

I was both lost and found; lost in a rage of hate and revenge, and newly discovered of the cynicism life imposes upon its suckers. Whether I might successfully enact the plan that was quickly taking hold in one side of my mind—to steal Roscoe's little gun and blow his head off—was beside the point. The other side of my mind had already concluded that whether or not I had the satisfaction of seeing his gushing blood flow deep into the cracked limestone, pumping out the last of his miserable life that seemed to have been conducted solely to confound my grandfather's happiness, whether I spat on Roscoe's grave or not, March was not coming back.

Jewel was once again alone and I was alone with her. The fishing trips on wild rivers, the backpack journeys into the high desert, all the things I would have done with my new father, grandfather, and friend, they were all just fodder for the conflagration burning hot inside me. Burning to a dry white ash that seared my tongue with the bitter taste of the way things really were and are and always will be: one big shit sandwich with just a little bit of bread and a whole lot of filling.

March had eaten his last, thanks to Roscoe; but Sandy still had to play out one more futile hole and the rest of his ill-advised life as if he had a chance. And that sorry son of a bitch Roscoe seemed to be enjoying every minute of it. That was the part that really pissed me off!

Roscoe was so confident now that he picked up his ball to allow Beast to finish the hole solo. Scooping out another big wad of his poisonous tobacco, he shoved it into his cheek.

"Ith over!" he mouthed through all that crap. "I win! Beasth could three-putt and I'd thill win!"

He was right. Sandy's ball had veered into the left rough, the most inhospitable piece of terrain on the course, and he was searching there among knee-deep weeds, wildflowers and little white rocks for his one lonely pellet. A month farther into the summer and the whole hillside would be dry and barren, but today the remnants of the wet spring were still working against him.

Still uncertain just how I could help Sandy, I found myself dragging up next to Beast in the fairway.

"Well, ol' March died with his spikes on!" said Beast, laughing like the heartless prick that he was.

Determined to say nothing, I bit down on my lip until I tasted blood.

Beast couldn't have been more than an eight- or nine-iron from the green. I pulled out his eight-iron and began to work on the grooves with his little file, tilting my hand first to one side and then to the other in an effort to round off the edges and take some of the bite out of the big man's clubs. Beast was still laughing at his little joke when it dawned on him that he'd been had.

"Hey! That deadbeat back there owes me five hundred bucks! Son of a bitch! Well, I'm gonna get it back on this last green!"

"Last green!" That's what March had said to me. Or was it? No, March wouldn't have told me what I already knew. It wasn't "Last green!" that he'd whispered. It was "Fast green!" He had meant that this was another of the slick greens like number two and number five, and the putts would roll across it like ball lightning down a mountainside! That was the message: his last wish. March was gone but he wanted me to help Sandy win. He wanted me to keep Roscoe from getting his father's land.

Beast looked me in the eye.

"Nine-iron," he said.

I choked down a dry swallow and handed him the eight that I'd been filing smooth.

Beast took the club. Then he reached out, grabbed me by the front of my T-shirt, and lifted me toward him. I was caught, and knew that I would soon be dead.

"What the hell is this?" he demanded to know.

I stuttered, trying to tell him it was an accident, that I had meant to hand him the nine. But the words would not come out.

"I told you to hold that file square," he bellowed. "Not at an angle! You trying to screw me up?"

I couldn't believe my ears. He still hadn't seen the number on the club, no real surprise considering he was holding me completely off the ground.

I'm flying! I thought, grinning like a fool in the big dummy's face. My feet don't touch the ground and I'm flying!

"You want your buddy Sandy to win, don't you?" he said, shaking me for an answer. Suddenly the truth was out and I was no longer afraid of him.

"Yeah!" I told him. "I do. I wish he'd beat you. I wish he'd beat you every round and every hole and every day of your life!"

"Well, why don't you wish in one hand and shit in the other and see which one fills up first," Beast suggested as he set me down. "It don't matter, Skinny. I'm gonna win, square grooves or not. Especially with these woolly greens. I'm Beast, legendary golf monster. Your buddy Sandy, he's just a legendary choke. Now watch this."

Beast wrapped his big paws around the grip of the eight-iron, made a perfect nine-iron swing, and sailed the ball toward the elevated green. From below the hill all we could see was the flag, but it looked to me like the ball had gone way long.

"Where'd that end up?" he demanded to know as he handed me the club.

I shoved it into his bag.

"Perfect," I said. "Right at the flag."

"All *right*!" he said. "That's what I been talking about!"

Sandy's ball was another story. From the tee I'd seen his shot hit a rock or root and bound straight left. Now he was looking in the wrong place; thirty yards from where I'd last seen the ball. Fromholz was walking around doing his best to help, but he was no closer.

"Two minutes, Fromholz!" Roscoe yelled from his cart in the fairway. "He's only got two minutes left to look for that ball. And that's *noocular* time!"

Roscoe started laughing at his joke and laughing at March and Sandy and at me. He was right too. Sandy was running out of time and that was something I couldn't let happen. If he didn't find that ball, Sandy would have to go back to the tee, move March's limp body to one side, and hit another drive. There was no way he had that in him. Even if he did, he still wouldn't beat Beast.

I dropped Beast's bag and started up the hill to help Sandy.

"Hey! Where you going?" Beast yelled.

I kept walking.

"If you help him find that ball, you can forget about getting paid!"

He kept yelling but I tuned him out and hurried toward where I'd last seen Sandy's ball. When I found it half-hidden under a little bush, my heart sank.

Even without the bush, the ball was in a terrible lie: half dirt, half caliche, and what seemed like half a mile from the green. There were several cedars about twenty yards ahead of him, which meant jumping the ball up fast, and there was a larger cluster of live oaks near the green, which meant carrying the shot a long, long way. Not that I hadn't seen Sandy hit some amazing recoveries. I mean he had just made a hole-in-one with the pressure on full throttle. I had once seen him almost hole one from a creek at Colonial. The ball had been completely submerged in three inches of water, and Sandy had come out of there covered by the sheet of mud and moss that his swing had raised, but by God, he made par! This situation didn't look nearly so promising.

You could almost hear Sandy's heart racing when I yelled that I'd found the ball. He came running, but as soon as he saw the situation, his excitement was replaced by the seriousness of the matter at hand.

"Billy," he said. "Get my clubs."

I walked back to where he'd dropped his bag, hefted it on my shoulder, and brought it to him as if I were his caddie. Actually, I guess I was.

"Whadaya think I should do?" he asked me.

I handed him his five-iron.

"Hit it sweet," I told him.

Sandy smiled at me, then he took the club. As he stepped up to the ball and began to search for the proper angle that would accomplish the required miracle, I began to hear a buzz in the air, a slight electrical mumble that I couldn't quite identify until I looked at Sandy's lips, barely moving as he whispered to himself.

"Guldahl Nelson Hogan, Mangrum Thompson Trevino, Sanders Zaharias Rawls, Haynie Whitworth . . . March . . . Bates . . ."

His lips slowly stilled, the sound of the mantra faded away, and Sandy took the clubhead back and up above his head. With the rest of his body almost motionless, his arms sliced the air and he picked the ball clean from the lie. It rocketed off his clubface, faded around the cedar trees and landed—I thought—somewhere near the green. Unfortunately, neither of us could see the target.

"Goddammit!" yelled Roscoe from the fairway, coughing on his chew for the second time that morning. "Goddammit, Beast! You better not let him beat you!"

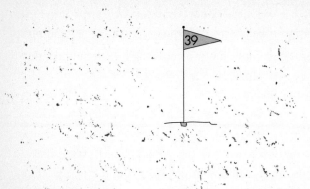

"I PICKED YOU 'CAUSE I wanted someone who knew how to carry a grudge!"

So March had spoken to Sandy earlier that morning. March would never know if he was right, but the rest of us soon would. After all the mighty drives, ripping irons, tender chips, and putts that "needed one more bean," after all the gamesmanship and trickery and spite, it had all come down to the flat blades: Sandy versus Beast, two quick rolls on a fast green for money and honor.

For Sandy, to make his twelve-foot putt and win the match would almost certainly mean redemption from the Beastly burden he'd borne on his shoulders for so many years. For Beast, the win literally meant salvation, the repaying of Benny Binion's Vegas loan sharks and a second chance at life, this time swearing only by the certain ball and club and never by the fickle dice. But instead of lining up his long putt from the back of the green, Beast was frantically searching through his bag for his last pack of butts, which I highly doubted he'd find, since they were in my pocket.

"What the heck?" I thought. "The guy smokes too much, anyway."

Finally he gave up the search, declined Roscoe's offer of a

chew, and began to nervously examine the downhill putt from all sides. Since I was now Sandy's caddie, I tried to stay as far from Beast as possible. As you'd expect, he was pissed about my having found Sandy's ball, pissed that the ball I'd found was now well inside his own, and pissed that I'd been screwing up the grooves on his wonderful irons.

The word *pissed* would have been far insufficient to describe his mood if he'd known that the main reason he was so far past the hole was that I'd given him the wrong club. I prayed that I'd left no telltale grass stains on the eight-iron (certainly all the other clubs were spotless, cleaned after every shot). He was also annoyed that I'd abandoned his bag for Sandy's. Having to carry his own bag was an atrocious thing to Beast. Figuring that I had lost his missing cigs, he no doubt blamed me for that also.

If this was bad for me, it was worse for Beast. What he needed to do was remember what he'd said about that other stuff not mattering anymore. It was all in the past, and a promising future lay in a good read of the slick downhill green and a sweet stroke right at the heart of the hole.

"Make sure it'll come up, asshole!" he told me as I tended the flag.

I pulled the pin from its seat, held it loosely in the center of the cup, and held my breath. It was a good stroke—not quite resembling his mechanical perfection on the putting green at dawn—but a smooth, steady roll, dead on line. If anything, the putt seemed a bit firm as the ball picked up speed moving down the slope. Growing larger as it came toward me, it began to gather momentum with the grain and the hill, refusing to break an inch in either direction.

I pulled the pin well clear and the speeding ball hit dead in the back of the cup, hopped into the air, and continued to roll about three feet past.

I stepped way back, close by the safety of Fromholz, as Beast silently marked his ball and turned his attention to Sandy. It wasn't over yet.

Sandy smiled to himself, even as he spoke to Beast. "Fast green, huh?"

Then, without even giving the putt another read, and certainly without consulting me, Sandy leaned gingerly over his ball and stroked it into the hole for a birdie and the victory. There was no pressure at all. It was almost as if he was winning dimes off his buddies at the practice green. The hollow rattle of the ball landing in the cup hung in the air a long time.

If March had only been there with us, Sandy's win would have been a jubilant and joyful occasion. As it was, no one spoke but Sandy.

"Shit!" he said, looking down at the putter in his hands. "I forgot to take off my glove! I *never* putt with a glove!"

MARCH'S CADILLAC, STILL SHINING in the grass by the first tee, could have been a flashy hearse for an eastside funeral. It occurred to me that we the respectful living should load him up and take him back to the Devil's Sanctuary for a West Texas funeral there by his daddy's grave. He'd won that land back, and I felt certain he'd have wanted to make the long journey home.

These thoughts rose briefly above the oppressive pall of my grandfather's death, then I turned again to the explosive situation that surrounded me. There still existed the very real possibility that March might not go to his grave alone. Sandy was the sole living winner and was about to walk away with the cash. That did not, however, discount the chance that Fromholz would try to collect the Vegas debt that Beast still owed to a group of men as close to being a Texas version of the Mafia as anyone would ever get.

By this time I had full confidence in Fromholz's ability to handle the situation and that was precisely the problem. With Beast's history of violent outbursts, he was liable to get himself shot down like a rabid dog, and I was scared shitless that I would either be caught in the middle or just plain have to watch it happen.

Looking back on it now, the interesting part of what took

place—all through the match perhaps, but certainly there in the parking lot—was not what happened, but why. On the golf course, I had witnessed the resolution of the past, the unraveling of a thirty-year-old mystery. In the parking lot, the final turn of the cards would reveal the future for more than one of our group.

The game hadn't been over five minutes, and already Roscoe and Beast were bickering as to whose shoulders should bear the burden of blame. Roscoe, of course, insisted that it was all Beast's fault for letting Sandy beat him. Beast alternated suggestions that the game was rigged with periods of brooding silence and a double dose of his usual profanities.

We arrived as a group at the three cars in the parking lot, Sandy's cheap Plymouth, Fromholz's black Chevy truck, and Roscoe's big Lincoln with the suicide doors.

"Okay," said Fromholz. "Ten grand of this belongs to Sandy."

Sandy took the cash.

"What about the rest?" Roscoe wanted to know. "What happens to March's wager? He's gone. I say we split it."

"It belongs to Billy," said Fromholz.

I could hardly believe it, and neither could Beast.

"No wonder that skinny piss-ant tried to screw me up all day!" complained Beast. "I protest the match!"

"Shut up!" Fromholz told him.

"No!" insisted Beast. "I ain't gonna shut up! That money's mine. I got screwed out of it and I want it."

I don't know how I could have been stupid enough to stray close to him, but as I peered into the bag of money that was being offered me, Beast reached out with one of his gigantic paws, grabbed me by my hair, and yanked me back toward him.

"The money's mine!" he repeated. In his other hand he brandished the jagged-edged shaft of his broken three-wood.

Fromholz shrugged as if this was either an inconvenience or a waste of time. Then he pulled out his big .357 Magnum and leveled it at the both of us, sighting down the barrel with his good eye.

"Beast," said Fromholz, "I'm gonna try my best to shoot your ear off. If I miss a little, I want you to know that it was my bad eye that made me do it."

There was a long and nervous pause as Beast considered his chances, which were slim and none. Then he released my hair, and I jumped away to safety.

"Crummy joke, huh?" Beast said feebly as he tossed down his broken weapon.

I knew I could count on Fromholz. I knew it. But then I noticed that in the distraction Roscoe had eased around to the back of his cart, opened the side pocket of his bag, and pulled out his little blue-steel automatic, which was now pointed at Fromholz.

"Okay, tough guy, Mr. Referee, bill collector, whoever you are: lose the gun."

What a hit man. Fromholz lets the guy get his gun out, lets him draw a bead on him, and then he does as Roscoe says. He lowers the .357 to his side.

"Now listen," said Roscoe. "March is dead. And as far as I'm concerned, I won. That's why I'm taking that cash. Blondie can keep his ten grand—he beat Beast—but the rest is mine. Now get out that deed and give it to me."

"There's a problem with the deed, Doc," said Fromholz as he passed it over. "March didn't sign it."

March wins again, I thought.

"*No problema*," said Roscoe with a laugh. "I been signing

March's name for thirty years. Matter of fact, I think I signed his name when we formed the company. I bet I can duplicate my own handwriting one more time. That land's gonna be worth a lot of money when the feds ram the new interstate through there. I don't believe March knew it, but with half of that land we were both wealthy men. Now I'm a real wealthy man."

"What about me?" Beast demanded. "Don't I get a share?"

"You don't get shit, big man!" answered Roscoe.

"That's right," said Fromholz. "But Roscoe, neither do you."

"Whadaya mean?" Roscoe demanded to know. "I got everything: the money, the land."

"You didn't get Jewel," I told him.

"Forget that bitch!" he told me right back.

Gun or no gun, there were some things I was not prepared to tolerate. March may have been my grandfather, but Jewel was my life, my family, my friend, my teacher and my chef; I had no intention of letting Roscoe talk that way. I ran full bore at him, my arms flailing like a windmill. I didn't need Fromholz. The gun meant nothing. Roscoe was an old man. I was young. If I couldn't kill him with my hands, I'd kill him with one of his own golf clubs. Two steps from him I felt a yank on my neck, my feet ran right out from under my body, and I was on the ground flat on my back.

Beast again, I thought. He's got me now.

Leaning my head back for an upside-down view of my attacker, I discovered not Beast but Fromholz. He was holding me by my shirt, now ripped halfway down the back. They were all against me, everyone. I fought to hold back my tears.

"Sorry, kid," Fromholz told me. "That was a distinctly bad plan you had there. Besides, Roscoe's going to apologize for insulting your grandmother."

"The hell I am!" said Roscoe, thrusting the gun into Fromholz's face.

"Oh, you're gonna apologize all right, Pops."

"Why should I?" Roscoe asked.

"'Cause if you don't, I'll kill you."

Roscoe laughed. "You got balls, Ref, but if there's gonna be any killing done, looks like I'm the one to do it."

"Go ahead," Fromholz told him, slowly raising his gun back to level. "Pull the trigger. Kill me! Kill me while you got the chance."

"You're bluffing!" said Roscoe.

"Pull the trigger, Roscoe. It's empty anyway."

A panicked look crossed Roscoe's face. As Fromholz leveled the .357, Roscoe squeezed on his trigger and it snapped down loudly on an empty chamber.

My entire body jerked at the loud click. There was a frozen pause all around, then Fromholz shoved the barrel of his big pistol into Roscoe's gut. The older man let out a painful groan.

"Sorry, Doc. I tossed your bullets into the pond at number three. Somebody mighta got hurt."

"*You* mighta got hurt!" Sandy said to Fromholz. "He just tried to kill you."

"Nah! He didn't pull the trigger till I told him it was empty. Ol' Roscoe's not a killer. He's just a bad loser."

"He killed March," I heard myself say.

"That's crazy talk!" said Roscoe.

Sandy came over and put his arm on my shoulders. "March had a heart attack, Billy. You were there."

"Roscoe stole his medicine!" I told them. "I put it back in the bag, but Roscoe took it out."

"Don't listen to him!" Roscoe pleaded. "He's just a kid."

Sandy went over to Roscoe's bag and began to dig around.

After a few moments he pulled out the missing prescription bottle with March's name on it.

"Shit!" said Sandy. "I'll settle this. Give *me* the gun."

Roscoe began stuttering excuses, which turned to confessions, and finally to a long list of apologies for which it was just too late.

"You got ten seconds," said Fromholz. "*Noocular* time, to get in that car and disappear forever."

"Wait for me!" begged Beast, pulling out his wallet and thrusting some bills at Fromholz.

"There's the fifty I won from March, and two hundred more. It's all I got, but take it. Tell Binion I'll pay the rest. I promise! He knows I'm good for it."

"Five seconds," said Fromholz.

Beast was still climbing head first in the window when the Lincoln roared off, the heat of the exhaust shimmering off the pavement as Roscoe's car disappeared beyond the hill that March's Cadillac had flown over at dawn.

Sandy and I were in shock. How could Fromholz have let a killer just drive away?

And that's when it happened. The trumpets sounded, the birds sang angelic symphonies, the gates of heaven swung open, and out popped the miracle of familiar speech.

"Morning, gents," came the voice. "Looks like you all got here early."

We wheeled around, and just behind us, standing arm in arm with Jewel, was William March: reprobate, poet, dreamer and friend.

I CERTAINLY NEVER KNEW I was a part of anything so grand or so well orchestrated. It was a con worthy of, and who knows, perhaps inspired by Titanic Thompson himself. I was not surprised to find that Fromholz was a part of the scheme, but Jewel's participation was almost more than I could fathom. Sandy, of course, knew even less about it than myself, and demanded to know why March had scared the shit out of us with that dying stunt.

"It was all your fault," said Fromholz. "After you shit-canned your drive on number nine, March was afraid you'd lose and I'd have to give the deed to Roscoe."

"You're not a hit man?" I asked Fromholz.

Fromholz and March both had a good laugh over that one.

"Billy, the only thing I hit," Fromholz told me, "is golf balls. I'm the assistant pro at the Las Vegas Country Club. You'll have to come visit me sometime."

"Neat!" I told him. "Can you teach me to shoot craps?"

"Over my dead body," said Jewel. "One dishonest golf game is bad enough. We won't be visiting any casinos, thank you."

I glanced at March and he winked at me. I knew then that someday we'd have some fun together in Vegas.

After all these years, I still wonder how March could have

known that I would do my part to help carry the day. I suppose he relied upon the fact that Jewel told him when the chips were down I'd do the right thing. I hope I did. There was a time when I thought I'd failed, but that was when I learned that the sky sometimes looks bluest from the bottom of a well.

I suppose the reason I've set all of this down is to testify that occasionally more saints are saved than sinners lost. That there are moments of salvation and redemption and, yes, sweet revenge, moments when despair turns to hope, and darkness dawns to gold, when absolutely all of life comes down to one final roll on a fast green, and the player with the steadiest hands gets to make himself a big fat sandwich with two thick slices of hot home-made bread and not one single iota of shit.

For once, when all of the settling of scores was done, despite the fact that I abandoned my employer to find Sandy's ball in a crucial moment, the caddie walked away well paid. For in his haste, Beast had left behind his square-groove clubs. And even though I learned to spin the ball backwards with them, I never enjoyed them as much as I enjoyed the thrill of handing Beast an eight-iron when he'd asked for a nine.

But I was a little wheel in a big machine. It had been Jewel's idea to bring Roscoe a bottle, Fromholz's four-wood had helped make an eagle, and of course the most important piece of the puzzle was our ace in the hole: Sandy Bates.

"I would have let you in on the con," March apologized to Sandy. "But I wasn't sure you could play golf and act at the same time."

"Play he did!" said Fromholz, adding the numbers on his scorecard. "Sandy was five under par for the nine: total of thirty-one."

"Thirty-one!" said Sandy. "Shoot, that's my lowest nine holes ever. I'd like to finish eighteen."

"The course record is sixty-three," I said. "You could beat that easy."

"Well," said March. "We've still got four sets of clubs."

"Me and Sandy against Fromholz and Grandpa!" I said, pulling off my torn shirt.

"Look out!" said Sandy. "It's the Wild Indian!"

The four of us were walking toward the number one tee, then March remembered Jewel and turned to her with his most beguiling smile.

"Jewel honey," he asked her. "Would you drive down to Mona's Restaurant to pick up some cheeseburgers for everyone?"

"Cheeseburgers?" she said in disbelief. "Cheeseburgers!"

I think for the first time in my life, my grandmother was totally flabbergasted.

Victorious, our foursome headed back onto the playing field with Jewel calling after.

"Bill March!" she said. "You get back here this minute!"

Bill March, I thought. What a grand name!

I turned to March. "Is she talking to you or me?"

March put his arm around my shoulder.

"Both of us," he said.

We walked on, together.

Epilogue

A LOT OF HOOKS and slices have come and gone since that memorable match, and knowing that I'd never be able to forget its participants, I've done my best to keep up with them.

Fromholz, who I first thought was a bad man, turned out to be a good man to have around, and despite his lack of peripheral vision, quite handy with his six-shooter against snakes of all kinds.

"Just call me Dead Eye!" he told me.

Now he owns a private poker casino in Vegas, where he personally deals the high-dollar games to rich suckers. The last time I visited him there I took in a few hands of cards and quit when I noticed that his longtime lady friend was winning most of the money.

In an ideal situation, I suppose Roscoe and Beast would have gone away wiser or more understanding, but if there's one thing I've learned, it's that nothing is ideal. Roscoe went on to the North Sea as head of the Glomar Explorer team and found a massive oil and gas field just where March's nose had indicated it would be. The last I heard of him, though, Roscoe had abandoned the cold and wet of Scotland for the sun and sand of Iraq. Soon after, war engulfed the country. Despite that, I can't help but think the old curmudgeon hasn't chewed—or swallowed—his last.

Carl "Beast" Larsen, I'm sorry to say, runs a driving range.

Sandy won the Texas State Amateur the year after our big match, and went on to qualify at the PGA school. Though he had toppled the giant and found the confidence his game was lacking, much to his disappointment, and my own, Sandy didn't make it when he went out on the Tour. He has, however, done just fine as a club pro these past twenty-some-odd years, and around the dinner table, carrots still become clubs and peas become balls as he tells his gaggle of blond-haired kids about his glory days competing against Arnie, Fat Jack and Beast, the golf monster.

As always, he still has a breathtaking swing. His greatest claim to fame is a remarkable accuracy on par threes. Thus far Sandy has recorded twenty-seven holes-in-one.

March, Jewel and I, after moving to the Devil's Sanctuary, reclaimed the Dry Devil's Golf Club and operated it as a public course until—as Roscoe had predicted—the federal government sliced it in half with four silver ribbons of asphalt. It was just as well. The town of Sonora built a more civilized course, and I didn't have to mow the grass greens March was planning.

And March? A dead man, it seemed, before the game began (and even more so before it concluded), I saw him reborn or rejuvenated or reinvented of himself, and it was only the ghosts that had haunted him that went to an early grave.

We took our trips on horseback and our long drives to Mexico and Montana, but we were always happy to get back to Jewel and her little adobe house overlooking the Dry Devil's River. I still see him there, that wink, that smile, both indicating that he knew something the rest of the world had missed out on. He was my grandfather, he became my father; and in his last bedridden months, I suppose he became my son.

There's no doubt in my mind that March really is playing matches on that big golf course in the sky. My guess is he's managed to team up with Francis Ouimet, Bobby Jones or Ti Thompson himself. Spotted one stroke too many, at the end of the round he collects the other team's halos or wings or golden putters, keeping them only long enough to polish them for another round tomorrow. Now that the Old Course at St. Andrews is open on Sundays, my guess is they sneak on for a little night golf.

Since March passed on a few years ago, my grandmother Jewel—whose unconditional love and patient wisdom held court over all—has assumed a respectable role in Sonora society where she continues to weave her charming magic to this very day. I drove out for the annual Wing Ding last summer, and there was a long line of wrinkled, leather-skinned old men waiting patiently to dance with her. Every one of them called her "Miss Jewel."

And me? With my hair already long, I became a part of the youth revolution of the sixties and abandoned golf for free love and Frisbees, both of which were a lot of fun. But the game of golf always knew that one day I'd come back. After an absence of almost ten years, one sunny afternoon I found myself parked by the side of a road, watching the foursomes come into the eighteenth green, and I knew it was time.

I've thought a lot about what's magic in the years since that fateful day: undying love, raising babies, playing eighteen holes without a three-putt. Now more than ever I wish that my lack of faith hadn't caused me to toss March's magic moon rock so deep into the woods. We could all use a little magic, even now, even those of us who are still able to count our friends as friends and our family as final.

As for my own son, Squirt—William March III—already he's surpassed me in getting out of sandtraps. I can only hope that my small fount of knowledge can keep up with his West Texas thirst for the unknown.

Sometimes we watch old westerns on TV, but we've yet to come across the one with the scene about what the white man and the red man know. Still, I've told him the story, and he has taken it to heart. We took a drive out into the Hill Country not long ago. I pulled over to enjoy the view, and he swept his hand across the horizon.

"See, Popi," he told me. "That's what neither of us know."

I haven't found him any moon rocks, but I am saving another even more important possession that March gave me. The inscription on the back of the photo is in the careful hand of a man who put his faith in salvation and sanctuary and the fact that no matter how far you wander, sooner or later, you will go home.

"Don't ever forget," it reads, "what an incredible journey we're on."

The photo may be old and worn, but it still shows two friends playing golf on horseback. March's was the Appaloosa.